In the Line of Fire

Daring Stories of Man's Best Hero

ACE COLLINS

Abingdon Press
Nashville

FX: 01-19

IN THE LINE OF FIRE
DARING STORIES OF MAN'S BEST HERO

Copyright © 2018 by Ace Collins

Library of Congress Cataloging-in-Publication Data has been requested.

978-1-5018-4186-6

18 19 20 21 22 23 24 25 26—10 9 8 7 6 5 4 3 2 1

MANUFACTURED IN THE UNITED STATES OF AMERICA

In the Line of Fire

More Abingdon Press Books by Ace Collins

Nonfiction

Man's Best Hero
Service Tails
Music for Your Heart

Fiction

The Fruitcake Murders
Hollywood Lost
The Color of Justice
The Cutting Edge
Darkness Before Dawn
The Christmas Star

Dedicated to Master Sergeant J. C. Burnam, whose service beside an amazing dog on the battlefields of Vietnam inspired four decades of work leading to the creation of The National Military Dog Monument.

CONTENTS

INTRODUCTION

There have been dogs on battlefields for thousands of years, but the first modern canine to be recognized as a full military partner by those with whom she served was a Civil War terrier. For four years this small bundle of fur and fire witnessed the horrors of war in some of the most remembered battles in history, and like the nation it changed her. In fact, from mascot to messenger to scout to sentry to sniffer, being in the line of fire dramatically transformed all the canines profiled in this book. It was that transformation that is the foundation for each of these remarkable and inspiring stories.

World War I, then called the Great War, was the first large-scale military operation to employ dogs as soldiers. In the war to end all wars a small mutt proved his courage on the battlefield and taught the world a lesson in loyalty that spanned two continents. In the most pivotal battle of World War I, a collie-greyhound mix gave everything he had to save France and in the process perhaps change the course of the entire war. There is also the all-but-forgotten story of an American soldier who rescued a puppy on a French battlefield. That simple act of compassion impacted the world of entertainment and changed the way dogs were trained in World War II.

Perhaps the book's most unlikely hero served with Canadians during the early days of World War II, while the most unusual and unexpected profile found in these pages is an Asian-born English Pointer that became the world's only official canine prisoner of war. Then there is the German shepherd born between French and German lines that flew on bombing runs with the United Kingdom's Royal Air Force.

Dogs were all but dismissed by the military when the Korean conflict broke out but a German shepherd that joined a legendary American unit would not only save hundreds of lives but also make such a huge impact that his service inspired an episode of the famed television series *M*A*S*H*. That canine hero also helped develop training methods used to educate thousands of dogs that served in Vietnam. While the canine heroes in that war performed gallantly and saved thousands of lives, they also suffered an unimaginable fate that still haunts many military veterans who once called these dogs partners. One of the canines profiled in these pages escaped that destiny while another did not.

The final two featured dogs, a springer spaniel and a German shepherd mix, have proved that canines are even more important in the technological age than they were a hundred years ago. Thousands of recent combat vets can attest that perfection is not just a military goal but, as seen in the service records of these two dogs, can actually become a reality.

From the Civil War to today the dogs featured in the pages of *In the Line of Fire* share a common thread: each exceeded expectations while adapting to unexpected situations. In doing so they proved the unimagined potential of God's most noble and loyal creation. These stories also seem to demonstrate that if mankind were more like man's best friend, there would be no need for military dogs as there likely would be no wars. But as long as men and women stand in the line of fire, surely a dog will be there too.

ONE

UNEXPECTED HEROISM

Heroism is endurance for one moment more.
—George F. Kennan

While dogs in our modern world fill many roles, a majority are still just pets and therefore their duties and responsibilities pale in comparison to what was expected by dog owners 170 years ago. In the middle of the nineteenth century, for those living outside cities, canines were indispensable. In reality, the dog was perhaps the most important family tool. It was not as much a pet as it was a sentry, hunter, herder, and defender. During an era when almost every rural family saw a dog as essential, it is interesting that canines served no official purpose in the military. It would take more than seven decades before dog training became a part of the military. Yet that didn't keep a feisty terrier out of one of the bloodiest battles in the American Civil War or prevent her from being recognized and saluted by the nation's most revered leader. To fully grasp the unlikely dynamics that brought this story to life, one first has to understand history as it unfolded.

By 1860, in the then not-so-*United* States, trouble had been brewing for more than a decade. But the event that set the stage for the breaking of a union was the election of Abraham Lincoln as president. In November the tall man from Illinois won the popular and electoral vote over a trio of competitors: John C. Breckinridge, John Bell, and Stephen Douglas. With Lincoln readying to take over the nation's highest office, those pushing for an end to slavery finally felt as if they had a strong and willing leader in power. Yet it was the fear that Lincoln would act quickly to emancipate the slaves that also created an environment where many in the South vowed to walk away from a nation that refused to recognize individual states' rights to determine whether one man could legally own another. While the newly elected president pushed for an understanding between the two factions, many in the media and in government deemed the nation already irrevocably broken. So in early 1861, even though few could fathom the deadly consequences that soon would drench American soil in blood, a clock was ticking, driven by moral choices that seemed to be anchored in stone. Soon that clock would hit the zero hour and when it did the country would blow up.

On February 8, 1861, a full month before Lincoln was sworn in, the slave-holding states officially left the union and announced the formation of the Confederate States of America. Not unexpectedly the government of the United

States did not recognize this new governing body. Yet war didn't break out immediately. Over the next few months, as the nation teetered on the brink of armed conflict, somehow, amid the fiery rhetoric, cooler heads prevailed. Thus many in the new president's administration actually believed the seceding states could be wooed back into the union without a single shot being fired. But those hopes were finally and forever dashed on April 12, 1861, when Confederate forces attacked Fort Sumter in South Carolina. For the next four years it would be brother against brother and father against son as more men died in combat than during any other American conflict.

A few weeks after the shots were fired at Fort Sumter, an unlikely hero was born. No one could have predicted that, more than a century and a half later, a brindle bull terrier would rank as one of the most remembered and cherished symbols of heroism and loyalty during the darkest period in American history. How this untrained canine came to symbolize the sacrifice and horror of war is one of the most unusual and dramatic stories of the Civil War. Yet even more amazing is the way this dog became a role model and inspiration for one of the country's most honored and revered regiments.

With the nation at war, the call went out for volunteers to engage the southern rebels. In communities across the Ohio Valley and up the Eastern Seaboard, tens of thousands signed up to wear union blue. With city bands playing patriotic songs, countless children waving flags, and city leaders making political speeches harkening back to the founding fathers' faith in a complete union of states and solidarity of the American people, the lure to join the military quickly built into fever pitch. These new soldiers had never experienced war. Most had not even been born when the War of 1812 ended. What they knew of battle was a product of books, plays, and family stories dipped in large doses of patriotism and glory and void of death and suffering. Thus, on the surface, war sounded like the greatest adventure known to man. In a very real sense, officers and newly enlisted men alike both saw the war as little more than a parade action.

In this climate, Colonel Thomas Gallagher, Lieutenant Colonel James Porter, and Major Samuel Jackson were directed to create the 11th Pennsylvania Regiment and within days more than a thousand men from throughout the commonwealth jumped at the chance to teach the Rebs a lesson. These passionate volunteers signed to serve just three months. Why? Because that was how long most predicted it would take until the South was tamed and peace was restored to the nation. With an easy victory seemingly ensured, on April 26, 1861, when the men of the 11th left West Chester and headed for Camp Curtin, Harrisburg, for training and organization, the mood was upbeat. Mothers weren't worried about losing sons and few of the men were concerned about dying in battle. In order to fully frame this upbeat and casual mood, a local citizen marched forward soon after the unit's creation with a five-week-old pit bull terrier puppy and presented it to Captain William Terry. This small helpless terrier seemed more a burden than a gift, but the captain readily accepted it figuring the dog would offer his men a diversion during training. The new recruits barked out possible names for their tiny mascot. Finally, after much discussion, the terrier was christened in honor of a beautiful local woman and the unit's colonel, Phaon Jarrett. Thus the tiger-striped pup, barely large enough to fit into a man's hand, became Sallie Ann Jarrett. At that moment of celebration no one could have predicted the horrific price of the war or that the dog's name would still be remembered and honored almost two centuries later.

By modern military standards, the training experienced by the men of the 11th might seem lax. On some days there was as much kidding around as there was teaching and drilling. Thus, there was plenty of time to spoil the growing pup. Using treats and kindness, many of the young soldiers attempted to win the favor of Miss Sallie. In fact, there seemed to be a competition to gain the undying loyalty of the unit's mascot. In those moments war seemed a million miles away and the men were more boys at summer camp than soldiers preparing to engage in a life-and-death struggle. Even when the regiment was assigned to the Army of the Shenandoah and shipped to Maryland, few sensed the horror that lay just over the horizon.

The 11th initially drew guard duty at Annapolis. A few weeks later they were moved to protect railroad lines in Manassas Junction. Both of these assignments gave the soldiers plenty of time to play with Sallie, and the growing pup was quickly trained to march in step when the men were on parade. With her ears pricked and eyes alert, she also was the first one up and in line for inspection when the bugler sounded reveille. Thanks in part to the mascot's antics and their relatively placid duty assignment, most of the men of the 11th still felt at ease. Yet, when the regiment was informed their enlistments had been extended from three months to three years, some began to fully grasp this was not a walk in the park; there was a growing chance they might actually face enemy fire.

As the sounds of war drew closer, as the men of the 11th observed the bodies of others coming back from battle, Sallie began to take on a role much greater than that of mascot and playmate. On long nights when gunfire and cannon blasts could be heard in the distance, the growing puppy became a living security blanket. As they slept on the ground, as tears of uncertainty filled their eyes, soldiers took turns holding this warm, breathing reminder of home and family. When they saw the terrier they were reminded of all they were missing. Thus, Sallie came to represent not only their own dogs waiting in Pennsylvania but also their families. In many of the letters the men of the 11th wrote, it was the terrier's exploits that drove the narratives. In the midst of war Sallie was delivering the love and devotion that mothers and wives could no longer give and the companionship and security once reserved for fathers.

By July, the letters home went beyond just highlighting

Sallie's tricks; they began to describe her personality. Those communications spelled out that the dog was affectionate and laid back. She also had no favorites, treating each member of the regiment with the same unbridled enthusiasm and now growled whenever anyone said "Rebel." She had also developed a nightly routine. She would visit each tent before heading to the officer's headquarters to bed down for the night.

One of the dog's most amazing qualities was witnessed during mess. She would not beg for food nor would she steal it, but she also made sure only those from the 11th got into the chow line. She would chase away any visitors who dared ask for grub. When the cooks or servers walked away from the mess tent, she allowed no one to get near the food stores. Somehow with no training she had become a sentry.

The fact that Sallie would not steal anything, even meat when she was hungry, became a teaching tool for officers. The dog was constantly singled out as an example of the honesty needed in order for the regiment to become a cohesive unit where each man could trust the other in and out of combat. Perhaps in part because of Sallie's example, the 11th became known for its character. Men could leave valuables in their tents and they would still be there when they returned. No one even cheated in poker. Officers from other units actually visited the regiment to uncover what kind of discipline was being employed to create this type of environment. They were mystified when the 11th's commander simply pointed to the bull terrier.

As the country prepared for its eighty-fifth birthday, the 11th was finally ordered to pack up and march to a combat zone. On July 2, 1861, after crossing the Potomac, the Army of the Potomac began to close in on General Thomas Jackson's Confederate Volunteers outside of Martinsburg, Virginia. As the lines were drawn and men checked and rechecked their weapons, the rural Virginia woods were calm. Birds sang, squirrels played in the trees, and a light breeze eased some of the summer heat, but for the first time Sallie was anything but subdued. She sensed something was about to happen and was nervous, wary, and anxious. While time slowed to a crawl and soldiers said silent prayers, Sallie raced from man to man, offering each a gentle nudge before moving to the next. When the order to advance was finally given, the terrier joined the flag corps and resolutely marched toward the Confederate forces. A few minutes later the placid calm was suddenly broken. As cannons fired and men yelled, peace gave way to terror. With no warning the troops were knocked to the ground by balls of lead and battle cries were all but drowned out by screams. Smoke soon brought haze as thick as a spring fog and in the man-made cloud the Grim Reaper was diligently seeking new victims.

As the battle continued and as the dog and the men tasted real war for the first time, Sallie stayed at her post beside the Stars and Stripes, watching anxiously as the soldiers she'd come to know and love were locked in a combat she couldn't have understood. The supposedly colorblind dog did somehow grasp something that would become even more evident throughout the remainder of her time with the 11th: those in gray were the enemy and whenever one of the Confederate soldiers drew close, the normally quiet terrier barked and growled. Sallie didn't stop until the invader was either pushed back or taken down.

After a few hours, the 11th's first battle was over as Jackson's forces were driven into a retreat. The now blood-drenched soil around Hoke's Run was claimed by the Union. On that summer afternoon ten of the men from Pennsylvania were wounded. As the doctors treated the injuries, Sallie went from soldier to soldier providing comfort and assurance. There was also one from the unit who died that day and the terrier spent extra time at his side. She urged him to get up and she likely couldn't fathom why he no longer responded to her voice. Yet as they took the dead man away for burial, the dog, along with those around her, seemed, for the first time, to understand the full price of war.

As many of the unseasoned men of the 11th would later reveal in letters home, it was Sallie's sense of duty and the fact that the eardrum-bursting noise of the battle had not driven her from her post that gave them the courage to keep fighting. Never once did the puppy flinch or take a step backward. Even with bullets sailing all around her, she remained steady. When the men around her moved forward, so did she. There were even times when she would dig a lead ball out of the dirt beside her, pick it up, and defiantly spit it out. Those who experienced their first taste of battle that July day would proclaim in letters home that it was Sallie that was the example of what each member of the regiment should strive to become.

That first battle, though not large in scope or staggering in losses, dramatically changed the 11th. The men had now witnessed death and had a part in taking lives. Watching a friend die and seeing others maimed had not just tested their character, it had altered their sense of reality. Though many were in their teens, they were now fully aware that death could come at any moment and that tomorrow was no longer guaranteed. Suddenly the glamor of war had been replaced with a grim sense of horror. On that July night, as they tried to find sleep, fear hung over their tents like a storm they couldn't escape.

Sallie made the rounds as usual. She went from tent to tent and silently offered her head for patting. She allowed troubled men to pick her up and hold her tightly in their arms. The terrier also solemnly studied the bed of the man who would not be coming back. Like the soldiers, on that night she slept fitfully. The next morning she was up before the signal for roll call and waited patiently for those soldiers who were healthy to join her. For the rest of her days in service Sallie would continue this routine of being the last to go to sleep at night and the first up each morning.

A bit more than a month later the 11th was sent back to the front lines. At the Battle of Cedar Mountain in Virginia, in the heat of August, the soldiers from Pennsylvania joined the Army of the Potomac to once more take on the Rebs. As man after man dropped, as cannonballs dug up huge mounds of dirt, and as rifles filled the air with lead, the terrier remained with the color guard. Then after the fighting ended, she made her way to the horrible and blood-soaked battlefield to inspect the bodies of the more than three hundred Union soldiers whose lives ended on that summer day. Well into the night she helped the death detail locate bodies hidden under brush and dirt. When those sober duties were completed, the dog made her way to the hospital staging area where she visited some of the fifteen hundred who had been wounded.

As the true horror of war sunk in, men wrote to their families about what they had witnessed. In many cases the most touching lines in those letters described the dog that seemed to understand and mourn for each man who had died at Cedar Mountain. The anxious and solemn soldiers also shared that when the dead had been buried and the wounded tended to, Sallie walked over to a hill, faced the direction of the Confederate lines, and mournfully cried. With that simple act she mirrored the thoughts and emotions of an entire nation that had come to realize that war was much more hell than glory.

The dog's unique reaction to war and adherence to duty continued at Thoroughfare Gap, Bull Run, Antietam, Fredericksburg, and Chancellorsville. Sallie courageously stood her ground during these battles and then served as a grief counselor when the hostilities ended. While the terrier's courage never wavered, her personality changed. The days of play had been replaced by a deep sense of loyalty and resolve. She seemed determined to greet each of the 11th's men every morning and stay as close as possible to them at night. She somehow understood they needed this bond.

With time, Sallie taught herself how to recognize the sounds of the enemy approaching and alert the men around her. She also began to somehow sense where cannonballs would be landing and with her frantic barks urged soldiers to roll away from that spot. These unique abilities seemingly gave Sallie a sense of invincibility. Thousands of bullets had struck within inches of her during the battles and she had not even been grazed. Thus, just before the start of hostilities, many in the 11th began to rub the terrier's head in an effort to "steal" some of her ability to dodge lethal fire.

Sallie soon became well known by those serving in the other units making up the Army of the Potomac and during lulls in the war men would walk miles just to meet the dog and share a treat. Once, a tall civilian in a dark suit visited the 11th. Upon seeing the dog, President Abraham Lincoln's sad eyes lit up. With hundreds of weary soldiers looking on, the nation's leader tipped his stovepipe hat in a solemn salute to the thirty-pound canine. Sallie seemed to understand the honor being bestowed as she rose up and held what appeared to be a salute.

By July 1863, the course of the war and the future of the Union was still very much in doubt and after two years of slogging through mud and snow, surviving heat and cold and dealing with unimaginable death and destruction, both sides were preparing for what would become the most monumental battle of the war. Back on home ground in Pennsylvania, the 11th readied for action at a spot just outside of Gettysburg. Their forces, lead by General George G. Meade, would take on the South's greatest military tactician, Robert E. Lee. One in four men who fought in this three-day battle would be seriously wounded or die. Those fortunate to survive Gettysburg would carry both mental and physical scars for the remainder of their lives.

Things did not start out well for the boys in blue. Soon after engaging the enemy, the 11th was overwhelmed and had to quickly retreat, leaving behind scores of dead. In an act that fully displayed Sallie's character and loyalty, she did not follow the flag corps to safety; instead she stayed with those who had fallen. As the enemy rushed past, the terrier went from one soldier to another. If she couldn't rouse them she moved on, but if she observed movement or heard a cry, she placed her head on the soldier's side and remained with that man until he died. For three long days, during which she neither ate nor drank, Sallie did not leave her post. She was still there with the Union dead when the Confederate forces retreated and the piece of ground once more became a part of the Union territory.

When the gunfire was finally miles away, a medical team arrived at the location where so many of the 11th had fought to the death. On what is now considered hallowed ground they found the dog. A burial detail later swore the dog was actually overcome with grief. As Sallie moved quietly from one body to another, it was like seeing a wife or mother attempt to deal with the loss of a loved one. Overwhelmed by what they observed, many of the hardened soldiers stood mute and cried.

Upon discovering Sallie was considered a member of the 11th, the officer in charge of the 12th Pennsylvania Regiment assigned a man to return the dog to the proper unit. On July 4, when that soldier tracked down the 11th, he discovered weary, beaten men whose faces reflected the sadness that had enveloped the entire nation. But when the exhausted soldiers spotted their mascot, they rose off the ground as one and rushed to meet the terrier. For three long days they thought she'd been killed. During that time they'd seen countless friends die as well. But on the day when a nation paused to celebrate its independence at least one prayer had been granted; Sallie was still with them. It was a moment that brought hope to men who had become completely hopeless.

For ten more months the 11th and Sallie soldiered on. On May 10, 1864, the regiment was back in Virginia engaged in a long and bloody battle at Spotsylvania. With Ulysses S. Grant now in charge of the Union Army, the North had the South on its heels. For those wearing gray, men and resources were running low and so was morale. Still against overwhelming odds, Robert E. Lee attempted to rally his men to fight on. Outnumbered two-to-one, the

Confederate soldiers battled hard at Spotsylvania, but it was for naught as the Army of the Potomac continued to drive the Rebels south.

As always, Sallie was with the flag corps. With her eyes turned toward the battle, soldiers in both blue and gray marveled at the canine's raw courage. Nothing—not noise, smoke, nor lead—rattled her. She was seemingly invincible. Then, in a moment that caused a shock wave across the Union lines, a bullet did what the men of the 11th believed was impossible; it pierced the dog's neck. As blood stained her coat, the stubborn terrier continued to hold her position. Only during a lull in the fighting did she allow a medic to treat the wound. By then she was almost too weak to stand.

For the next few days the soldiers who served with the dog watched and waited to see if their mascot and morale officer would be able to beat the odds and survive. During those long days they fed her the best from their rations and took turns sitting by her bed. They also prayed over the dog and encouraged her with gentle pats and kind words. And somehow, by the time Grant drove Lee out of Spotsylvania on May 20, Sallie was up and ready to march with her fellow soldiers in pursuit of the Rebs.

Sallie and the 11th next met the enemy in North Anna and then in Cold Harbor. Week by week and month by month they pushed forward against the tattered remains of the Southern Army. Then in the dark, gray days of winter, the war-weary men from Pennsylvania faced a badly outnumbered group of Southerners at Hatcher's Run,

Virginia. On February 6, Sallie moved forward as the first line of Union troops advanced on Confederate positions. The fighting was fierce and close with men involved in hand-to-hand combat. It was a soldier's worst nightmare come to life. Over the sounds of battle one could hear the screams of the dying and within an hour the ground was littered with the dead and wounded from both sides. As a second wave of Union soldiers rushed in to reinforce the 11th, a soldier stumbled across Sallie. Her eyes were open but unseeing. The terrier had died instantly and alone. She had one wound to her head.

In the midst of what was described as a solid wall of lead, word was passed that the 11th's mascot had been killed. Even in the heat of the battle, as they fought in a life-and-death struggle to survive, grown men cried. A few became so possessed by grief they even tossed down their weapons and retrieved shovels from their packs. Oblivious to the bullets hitting on all sides, those determined soldiers rose to their knees and began to dig a hole in the middle of the battlefield. Miraculously, in the minutes it took to create that small grave no one was hit. After the work was completed, one soldier crawled to the spot where Sallie had fallen, gently picked up her lifeless body, and brought it back to the freshly dug hole. With the battle raging, this volunteer burial team said a prayer, lowered Sallie into the ground, and covered her body with dirt. Then a bugler, one of those she had stood beside for years, rose and courageously played "Taps." After placing a cross and a small flag on the grave, the men went back to the fight, but as many would later tell their families, their tears clouded their eyes for hours and when they looked toward the flag corps they openly wept.

In less than two months from the moment Sallie was killed in the line of duty the war ended and the Union had been saved. Of the 1,890 men who signed up to serve in the 11th Pennsylvania, only 340 marched home. Few of them would ever speak of the horrors they witnessed on the battlefields, but almost all of them would continue to share Sallie's story.

In 1890, on the twenty-fifth anniversary of the end of the Civil War, many of the surviving members of the 11th dedicated a monument at Gettysburg. This granite marker looked a bit different than all the others lining that sacred piece of American landscape. On the top was a statue of a Union soldier representing all who fought for the regiment but at the base was the bronze likeness of a bull terrier whose courage, love, and loyalty inspired the men every step of the way. Though never officially a member of the military, Sallie Ann Jarrett surely earned the title of America's first canine war hero and thus built the foundation and set the benchmark for all those dogs that would follow.

Two

No Limits

The limits of the possible can only be defined by going beyond them into the impossible.

—Arthur C. Clarke

Often history is shaped and defined by seemingly mundane or insignificant events. The unlikely heroes that emerge during these make-or-break moments can provide inspiration for decades. Many even become the stuff of legends. Over a century ago the exploits of a dog named after the devil likely saved not just thousands of lives, but perhaps the fate of an entire nation. It was in the midst of the worst battle of World War I that Satan flew as if on wings of angels straight into the hearts of men and women all over France. Interestingly, it was human failing that set the table for this incredible story.

In 1914, a series of circumstances came together to soak European soil in blood. The foundation for the Great War, as it was called then, began with a massive arms race between the world's greatest powers, with the weapons being developed and manufactured in the early twentieth century being far more lethal than any the world had yet known. Across Europe the last vestiges of monarchies trying to hold on to power were coveting tanks, airplanes, powerful artillery guns, and poison gasses. The leaders from democracies joined this frenzied sprint for power by rationalizing that these new technologies offered the best chance to maintain peace. If the arms race had been the only issue facing the Western world, coolheaded diplomats might have been able to avoid war. But there was something else at work that made conflict all but inevitable.

At the heart of the mistrust gripping Europe was nationalism. Ethnic loyalties heightened suspicions between neighbors, fueled angry and volatile newspaper editorials, and resulted in oppressive legislation. Nationalism also drove countries to form alliances guaranteeing if one nation went to war then all the treaty signers would go to war as well. Thus, it only took one seemingly minor action to trigger a war such as the world had never seen. Strangely, that trigger would literally be pulled far from where the major battles were fought. In fact, almost all those who would give their lives in this worldwide conflict had never heard the name Ferdinand until June 28, 1914.

For more than a decade there had been a series of riots and assassinations in the Balkans. On a warm Thursday afternoon, Archduke Franz Ferdinand visited Sarajevo, Bosnia, where Serbian revolutionaries, driven by ethnic pride, made an attempt on the archduke's life. It failed and most of those responsible were arrested, but the few who escaped did not give up. After the archduke visited those who had been wounded in the initial attack, a remaining conspirator, Gavrilo Princip, struck again and this time the assassination was successful. And because of the many confusing and convoluted alliances the death of a seemingly insignificant and almost unknown leader shook a continent's foundations.

In the unsettling weeks that followed, diplomats shuttled between European capitals trying to head off a full-scale war. However, by late summer their efforts—thanks to suspicions, jealousy, and nationalism—were doomed. By August a conflict broke out that would eventually take the lives of ten million men. In this new technologically fueled war all rules were tossed off the table, and in a strange time when horses and tanks were used side by side, the past and present collided and men died in ways that would have been unimaginable just a decade before.

Though almost every nation in Europe would quickly become involved, a large portion of the war played out on a stage between Germany and France where men in foxholes lived and died in the mud. It would be an almost year-long battle around the French city of Verdun that would eventually determine the outcome of what we now know as World War I and the hero that turned the tide of history was not a general but a black dog.

The demonic nature and cruelty shown during the battle for Verdun caused the press to refer to the conflict as the Devil's War. The men who fought in those trenches christened the battle "the Furnace." It was their polite way of calling the battlefields around the small French town "hell on earth."

By the time Verdun became the staging point for the key battle in the "War to End All Wars," it was more than a thousand years old. Throughout history this small town had hosted battles and seen its share of death, but never anything like what was recorded in 1916. The kaiser and his army felt that if they could inflict enough suffering at Verdun then the French would capitulate. Thanks to this philosophy the sun was always obscured by smoke, poison gases floated through the air like a London fog, and death became so common that it had no sting.

Before World War I began, dogs were used by the military only as mascots. Yet during this war both sides trained thousands of canines for a wide variety of duties. The French even set up schools to educate their army of dogs. The animals in these training centers were products of almost every large and medium-sized breed and were instructed based on their intelligence and athleticism. Depending upon their assigned duties the four-footed soldiers spent four to eight weeks in school. A majority of the graduates became guard or enclosure dogs. They were essentially sentries that warned of approaching intruders.

The French also sent a small number of dogs through detective school. These canines were used for tracking down spies and deserters as well as locating injured men on the battlefield.

Because of a shortage of horses and mules as well as trucks, the largest canines were assigned to pull carts containing needed equipment, food, and medical supplies.

An elite group of dog school graduates was given the most dangerous duty: liaison or carrier dogs. They were expected to transport messages when all other forms of communication were down. In their assignments they would have to race through poison gas, gunfire, and minefields. As the Germans could readily see the metal message tubes on the dogs' collars, they were also prime targets. Thus, hundreds were killed before completing their first mission.

Two years into the war, an animal trainer named Duval was assigned to the war school at Satory, France. His task was to prepare an Irish setter named Rip and a friendly collie-greyhound mix ironically christened Satan. This unique duo was destined to serve as carrier dogs.

During World War I, basic training for dogs was even more demanding than it was for men. Over the course of eight weeks Duval put the animals through their paces. He began with general obedience work and then progressed to creating a strong personal bond with the animals. As he would be going to battle with the animals they had to be able to respond to his voice and follow his commands no matter what was going on around them. So maintaining a singular focus was essential.

After undying loyalty was established, the classroom shifted to real battle situations where live ammunition and the sounds of bombs filled the air. Once the dogs passed this portion of the course work, Duval devised a training method meant to enhance Rip and Satan's ability to dodge enemy snipers. Rather than have them run straight to him, Duval taught them to race in a zigzag pattern. When a bullet struck near the dog, the trainer ordered them to change direction. Once the two canines had mastered this method of avoiding fire, Duval placed them into a field with foxholes, artillery craters, smoke, and even poison gas. There they learned to climb and jump through and over trenches, note and run from gas, and even hide from gunfire until things cooled down. Trying to foresee every possible battle situation and re-create it, the trainer put the pair through their paces both day and night. Nothing stopped their education. They even worked in rainstorms and snow.

When they weren't training, Rip and Satan were always at Duval's side. They ate with him, slept beside his bed, and followed him everywhere. By the time their education was completed, they were as much Duval's children as they were tools of war.

When Duval arrived at Verdun, the battle had been raging for months. The first shots were fired in February, and from there the war spiraled through spring and was now raining bloody terror in the summer. All around the town were the signs of destruction. The city's children had seen so much death they were numb. They no longer reacted to carts filled with bodies or the pleas and cries of the wounded. It seemed this living hell had become such a normal part of their world it no longer made an impact.

As he inventoried the sad lives of Verdun's children, Duval came to realize he could make an impression on the little ones in two ways. The first was with food. The civilians in this city were not just tired, they were hungry. So sharing a piece of candy or a bit of meat with a child brought a small bit of hope.

The other method for making a positive statement was through the dogs. As soon as the kids spied Rip and Satan they raced toward them, hugging the animals as if they were long-lost relatives. Duval soon learned the horrific reason the children viewed Rip and Satan with so much wonder and excitement. The area's dogs had disappeared. Many had been killed in battle, some had starved, and others had become food for desperately hungry families. Thus, the pets the area had once treasured were all but gone.

Beyond the children, Rip and Satan also offered war-weary soldiers a chance to escape for a few minutes. It seemed that for men who'd been on the battlefield for months, petting a dog brought about a sense of security and comfort even in the midst of flying bullets and floating gas. The unconditional love offered by the Irish setter and collie mix created some peace in the midst of hell on earth, even if just momentarily.

As a trainer/soldier, Duval's first job was to find someone at the garrisons who could take proper care of the dogs. Once these handlers were identified it was time to teach Rip and Satan the "road" between where they were stationed and where Duval would be headquartered. The trainer set up his operations at Thiaumont, a small town that had changed hands sixteen times in the first few months of the battle but was now held by the French. During lulls in battles, Duval taught the dogs to run from their assigned garrisons to Duval's location at battalion headquarters. Once he was sure the four-footed soldiers had learned the course, the trainer left Rip and Satan with the handlers.

The jet-black Satan was assigned to the garrison at Verdun. Rip joined another group not far from a point near the front line. Over the course of the first month of duty, Satan would complete a half a dozen missions carrying messages back to Duval. Those communications would include information on German positions and current French needs. After a day with the trainer, Duval would then have the black dog return to this group.

Satan's grace, power, and speed soon became the talk of the war. American war correspondent Albert Payson Terhune, who was already the world's best-known dog writer, wrote newspaper stories of the canine's amazing abilities. This burst of fame would be noticed by those supporting France as well as the Germans. The latter put a price on Satan's head. Thus, because of the collie mix's record of success, each new mission became more dangerous and more difficult.

When a German sniper killed Rip, a distressed Duval turned his full attention to Satan. The wiry man with the solemn expression spent extra time training the collie mix to run closer to the ground, to seek out the safety of foxholes when under fire, and to always move in a zigzag line even when he was not under fire. While this additional training might have increased Satan's odds for survival, it didn't ease the trainer's concerns.

It was when the phone lines went out that Duval became most anxious because he knew the men at Verdun only had three choices for communication. One was to use the pigeons, the next was to send a man, and the third was Satan. On those long days Duval always made his way as near as possible to the front line where he would nervously pace the trenches while he waited for his dog. Somehow Satan always survived the hail of gunfire to complete his missions.

On the nights that Duval had Satan, the trainer was bombarded with questions about the animal's ability to literally dodge death. Many observers suggested luck was the reason the dog had survived, but Duval always framed his responses with logic. He painstakingly explained that the dog happily sleeping at his feet was the accidental product of breeding. With the room silent and all eyes focused on the heroic canine, the trainer pointed out that by combining a tri-color collie with a greyhound, Satan was graced with both incredible speed and intelligence. He didn't as much react as he assessed a situation and adapted his training to adjust to it. His speed, along with his ability to adapt and learn, were the major reasons he had never been stopped. Duval finally pointed out the dog's midnight-black coat that had given him his name made him all but invisible at night. When pressed, the trainer also admitted that Satan was the smartest animal he'd ever known.

In late fall, as the weather cooled and the German offensive heated up, Duval left Satan behind at battalion headquarters and traveled to visit the garrison at Verdun. The men he met that day appeared years older than they had just a few weeks before. Thin, tired, and discouraged, the soldiers were living in holes on a landscape that was so bombed out it might as well have been the lunar surface. And everywhere there was the smell of arsenic. Because of the increased use of that and other poison gas, the soldiers were spending as much time with their gas masks on as they were breathing unfiltered air. At this moment, Verdun had to have been the most depressing and foreboding place on earth.

Not long after the dog trainer entered the camp, the Germans launched another fierce offensive. Overwhelmed and outnumbered, the few hundred French soldiers were quickly surrounded. When the telephone lines were cut, the garrison's frantic calls for reinforcements ended. As more lethal gas rolled in and the heaviest artillery fire of the war pounded Verdun, the Frenchmen found themselves completely cut off from the world. Their first instincts demanded they retreat, but the men knew that if Verdun fell the war would likely be lost. So in the face of almost sure death, they held their position out of loyalty to France.

One day gave way to a second as the men valiantly found a way to survive. As they stubbornly hung on, they sent out the pigeons one by one carrying urgent messages seeking help. Snipers brought down each bird before it had flown a hundred yards. Two dogs were sent out next where they met the same fate. Finally with scores now dead and with the company's food almost all but gone, the call went out for human volunteers. With hundreds of hopeful, praying, and exhausted men looking on, the first volunteer jumped out of the trenches and raced toward headquarters. He was shot and killed less than a hundred feet into his mission. Over the course of the next day, six more men tried to race through the gauntlet of fire with none of them making it more than a few hundred yards.

Even if the French soldiers trying to hold onto Verdun had never read the story of the Texans at the Alamo, they had to be sure of the fate that awaited them. In order to destroy the will of the people of France and their government, these weary men knew the Germans would show no mercy. It was therefore natural that many of the stranded and hopeless men began to write last notes to loved ones while others fell to their knees and prayed. Among these seeking divine help was the dog trainer Duval, who now believed that without a miracle he was doomed to die without the animal he so loved.

Miles away at the headquarters no one was aware of the plight of those at the Verdun garrison. Yet when the Germans dramatically increased their artillery barrage aimed at the small town, the commanders grew concerned. In an attempt to learn what was going on, pigeons were sent out. The birds were shot down almost as soon as they left the ground. As officers paced back and forth and discussed what could have been happening at Verdun, some offered the opinion that it might be best to retreat. Others argued that retreating meant essentially surrendering to the Germans so they had to hold on for the future of France. As the room went silent a man made a suggestion, "Duval is at Verdun; let's send his dog with a message. If only for their own morale they at least need to hear from us and we must know what is happening so we can understand how to respond."

A few minutes later when Satan, eager for duty, was brought into the room, seasoned military men wondered if this unlikely animal held the future of France in his paws. For several minutes the officers discussed the situation, trying to come up with another option, but no fresh ideas surfaced. Finally the commander picked up pen and paper, wrote a very short note, and placed it into the metal tube on the dog's collar. The officer then asked his assistant to retrieve two carrier pigeons. Once the birds had been brought to headquarters, they were placed in wire cages and strapped onto Satan's back. If the dog made it to Verdun then perhaps one of the pigeons could fly back with a note communicating what was going on at the garrison. A knock brought all eyes to the door. A soldier entered with grim news.

"The Germans have gassed everything between here and the garrison. The dog won't last more than a few hundred feet before dying."

If times had been different this would have been the death knell for the mission, but with the entire war on the line, the impossible had to become a reality. An officer took his own gas mask and pushed it over Satan's head. It took some time and extra straps before the life-saving device was secured. Surprisingly the dog didn't try to pull the mask off. Instead, he walked resolutely out of the room with a handler who led Satan to the front lines. Following a network of trenches, the pair drew as close as possible to the objective. Then with hundreds looking on, the black dog was lifted out of the trench and urged to go find Duval. As German gunfire picked up and explosions lit up the night sky, Satan, looking like a creature from another world, took a second to gain his balance and then lunged forward. Zigzagging down a bombed-out road, he quickly gained speed while exhibiting a singular purpose to complete his mission.

The first mile and a half of Satan's trip to the garrison offered uneven terrain, mounds of dirt created by explosions, and even a few thick bushes. Those who watched him until he finally disappeared noted the dog sought out the cover, waited until gunfire calmed down, and then ran to the next place offering safety. Though there were no eyewitnesses once he was lost in the darkness, the dog likely continued the pattern he had been taught by Duval until about a half mile from his destination. At that point the cover disappeared and Satan was facing an open stretch of flat ground. With the sun now coming up there was no place to hide.

It was a sentry at Verdun who first noted a black shape hugging the ground while running in a random meandering fashion toward the garrison. The man readied his rifle as he called out for others to join him.

"What in the world is it?" one asked.

With the gas mask over his face and the birdcages strapped to his back, Satan looked like a huge-headed monster. As the imposing figure grew closer some even wondered if a demon was approaching. Finally, one of the soldiers recognized the creature as a dog and with the Germans now concentrating their fire on the animal he assumed it had to be one of their own.

"It's Satan!" a man screamed. "Get Duval!"

When Duval arrived and peeked over the edge of the trench he must have sensed a combination of relief and fear. His dog was performing perfectly, doing everything he had been taught to avoid the snipers' fire, but there was still two hundred yards between the collie mix and safety.

"Come on boy!" the trainer screamed.

As if inspired by the familiar voice, the dog shifted into another gear. Satan now seemed to be moving so fast it appeared as if his feet were barely touching the ground. Then with hundreds of hopeful eyes looking on, a German bullet found its mark and the black dog fell motionless to the earth.

Tears filled the Frenchmens' eyes as they watched their canine comrade lying on the ground. Completely overcome with shock and grief, Duval screamed what all of them must have been thinking: "No!"

That word had no more than cleared the trainer's lips when Satan struggled to his feet and stood. As blood seeped from his shoulder, he regained his bearings and began to move forward, but he was no longer running; now he was staggering like a drunk. Just a few steps after rising Satan took another bullet in the leg. He wavered momentarily before pitching forward and sinking to the ground.

Seemingly possessed, Duval climbed out of the trench. With the Germans now concentrating their fire on the crazed man, the trainer screamed words that would forever be remembered by all those at Verdun. "Satan. Have courage my friend. For France!"

As a completely exposed Duval watched his dog, now only fifty yards away, struggle to his feet, a dozen snipers pulled their triggers simultaneously. Six of the bullets found the trainer. He swayed and looked once more at Satan before tumbling back into the trench. While this move would cost Duval his life, the distraction gave the dog the opportunity to complete his mission.

Hobbling on three legs, Satan slowly and painstakingly pushed toward the French line. When he was within ten feet, three men bravely crawled out of their trench and grabbed the dog's collar, pulling him to safety just before another barrage of bullets filled the air. Too weak to stand, Satan lay unmoving as the message was yanked from the tube and the bird cages were stripped from his back. After his gas mask was removed, Satan crawled forward toward Duval's body. The exhausted and badly wounded dog nuzzled his trainer's hand while the garrison commandant read the message.

For God's sake, hold on. We will send troops to relieve you tomorrow.

Taking paper and pen, the man in charge scribbled two identical notes giving information to headquarters on the location of the German artillery unit. He then secured the notes to each of the birds' legs and released the pigeons. One bird was shot down but the other managed to fly through a wave of fire and make it home. An hour later, using the coordinates in the message, long-range guns took out the German battery encamped on the ridge above the town. As Albert Payson Terhune would write in a newspaper story from the front, "The garrison was able to hold out until reinforcements came all because one hairy mongrel refused to die while his errand was still uncompleted."

With their artillery severely damaged, the Germans quickly retreated. When they pulled back to regroup, the entire face of the war changed. The Allies, who had been hanging on by a thread, now moved forward on an offensive. The Germans would fight hard for another year but not mount a real challenge. Yet the damage inflicted in the twenty-five thousand acres around Verdun would never be completely healed. In a place where more than a million died, the earth remains so poisoned it is still a lifeless, barren wasteland filled with thousands of yet unexploded shells.

There are no records on what happened to Satan after this mission. Decades later a few sources reported the dog recovered from his wounds and lived his remaining years as a pet. In truth, this tale was likely created for the children of France to assure them their revered canine hero's story ended happily. As there is no official notation of Satan ever serving again and no soldiers' letters mention him, it is far more likely that after completing the mission that turned the tide of the Great War he died next to Duval.

No matter where or when he drew his last breath, Satan's legacy can never be questioned. He changed the military's viewpoint of the potential of dogs and with his courage and loyalty inspired a war-weary nation to continue fighting. In a very real sense, Satan became France's canine angel and the dog that saved a nation.

Three

Loyalty

I take things like honor and loyalty seriously. It's more important to me than any materialistic thing or any fame I could have.

—Lloyd Banks

During the American War for Independence, it was the French who first came to aid the fledgling United States. Many historians believe that without French support, the British would have won the war. A century and a half later it would be Americans coming to French soil to help fight the Germans that turned the tide of what was then known as the Great War. During these dark moments in history an American soldier would forge a personal alliance with a French-born subject forming a bond of loyalty that reached from Paris to Chicago and still resonates as one of the greatest war stories of all time.

The United States entered what we now know as World War I in April 1917. One of those shipped to Europe to fight "over there" was Private James Donovan. Except for his Midwestern roots and lack of family, very little is known of Donovan before he joined the service. Yet though the details of his personal life might be sketchy, his military record is much more comprehensive. Assigned to the 7th Artillery, he was trained as a communication specialist and spent most of the war on the front lines stringing or repairing telephone wires. He was a constant target of enemy snipers, gas attacks, and artillery barrages as he worked tirelessly in the summer heat and the bitter cold winter of 1917.

At about the same time Donovan arrived in France, a litter of mongrel pups was born in Paris. This was a time when food was scarce and families were forced to give up their pets, thus dogs of all breeds and sizes roamed through city streets and the rural countryside. Many were seen as nuisances and shot on sight. Some starved to death. The lucky hounds somehow found enough scraps to eke out a day-to-day existence.

In the coldest French winter on record, a fifteen-pound mutt, it's wiry, unkempt hair grayish in color, searched trashcans for food and sought out coal bins for shelter. On a regular basis the small dog was cursed by shopkeepers and constantly driven away from their businesses. He was certainly chased by dogcatchers and probably kicked by pedestrians. The mongrel rarely felt the touch of a friendly human hand. As winter gave way to spring and the nameless tiny dog avoided the machinery of war clogging the narrow Paris streets, he continued his personal battle to survive. Yet as food became scarcer, the odds of survival grew slimmer with each passing day. By summer the flea-covered mutt was little more than skin and bones.

A year into the war, Private Donovan had impressed his superiors enough to be raised in rank and chosen to represent the US military in a July 14, 1918, Bastille Day parade in Paris. This assignment provided a welcome break from dodging gas and bullets and a chance to finally see the City of Light. When the festivities concluded, Donovan and Sergeant George Hickman opted to stay in Paris for a few more hours. After viewing a few of the sights, they headed to a café. While eating a welcome hot meal and enjoying the live music, they lost track of the hour. By the time they walked out of the café, it was hours past the time they were to report to their units. Compounding the serious problem of being AWOL was that darkness now hid all the city's landmarks so they had no idea what direction would take them "home."

While walking through an alley, the soldiers saw what appeared to be a small pile of rags. As they strolled by, it moved. Stopping and leaning in closer, Donovan carefully studied what he quickly discovered was a pitiful gray, white, and taffy colored dog. While it showed no fear, it also didn't eagerly greet the men. Instead it remained cautious as if reading their body language.

Donovan was still holding a piece of pastry and in an act of compassion offered it to the dog. The mutt quickly gobbled it down and then shifted his focus back to the men as if watching to see if any other treats would follow. With nothing more to share, the American soldiers turned and continued their now anxious search for something that could guide them back to their unit.

The brutality of the Great War made desertion a major problem. The military police regularly patrolled Paris and the surrounding areas to uncover soldiers who'd grown so weary or so frightened they had walked away from their posts. On that long-ago summer night it was an MP who discovered Donovan and Hickman. In an accusing voice he demanded to know why they were in the city. He was not impressed with their explanation and pointed out that other Americans who had marched in the parade had returned to their units hours before. Donovan admitted that while they had stretched their adventure out a bit, neither was a deserter. They were just lost.

The MP cautiously eyed the pair for several moments before noting the ragged dog sitting a few feet behind them. After studying the hapless creature, the military policeman asked Donovan if the mutt could verify their story. It was at that moment the soldiers told their first fib and in the process literally set in course a partnership that would save the lives of hundreds if not thousands of American soldiers.

"Rags is the 7th Field Artillery mascot," Donovan explained, "and we're escorting him home."

"Fine," the MP answered. "I'm a dog lover myself. And to make sure Rags makes it back to the unit I'll lead you there."

In an attempt to keep their escort happy, over the course

of the next few miles Donovan and Hickman took turns holding the dog they had just christened Rags. They also no doubt embellished the story of what the mutt meant to the unit. The ploy worked as the canine refugee literally saved the men extra duty and a reduction in rank. It would not be the last time Rags pulled Donovan's tail out of the fire.

For the next few days the 7th remained well behind front lines so Donovan had plenty of spare time to get to know his new canine friend. Though still not eager to be petted or coddled, the dog recognized Donovan as a meal ticket. Because he continued getting a share of the soldier's rations, Rags became the American's shadow. When division headquarters was moved to the front, Rags followed Donovan step for step. As he got his first taste of war, the dog dodged fire while accompanying his human friend stringing new communication lines between the 26th Infantry and the 7th Artillery. When those lines were knocked out by enemy artillery fire, which happened several times, Rags and Donovan then went out to fix them.

After a week of combat action and a number of close calls with death, Donovan had grown to love Rags to the extent that his concern over the dog's welfare was stealing his focus on his job. Thus, when he had a few hours off, Donovan walked his four-footed companion several miles back to headquarters. Once there, he convinced another soldier to feed and care for the animal, then, after sharing a final treat and rubbing the little dog's head, he headed back to the front lines.

Over the next couple of days Donovan grieved. He also found that not having Rags with him as he went about his dangerous assignments actually made him more apprehensive. At night, as he counted his blessings for surviving another day at the front, the loneliness was even more profound. Donovan wasn't the only one wishing the dog was still around. Others in the 7th missed Rags almost as much. Thus, conversations often turned to the mutt and many involved his questionable lineage. Some pointed to the ears and tail and suggested there was some French poodle in the canine's family tree, while others felt the head was all terrier. Certainly the character Rags had displayed was much more ingrained in the latter rather than the former. A few even suggested they had seen a bit of Scotty in the dog. Yet Donovan and his friends would soon discover that there must have been a bit of homing pigeon in Rags as well. One afternoon, when he was stringing wire in no man's land, the soldier looked around and saw Rags coming up the hill. It appeared the dog cared much more about the love of a man than the fear of death.

Now realizing Rags had made his choice and would be his for the duration, Donovan opted to educate the dog to perform like a real mascot. This worthy goal proved to be an exercise in futility. Donovan spent hours trying to teach Rags tricks. The dog had no interest in sitting, barking on command, playing dead, or fetching. The fact that he wouldn't learn put the dog's position with the unit in peril. Most commanding officers didn't like dogs on the front and this was doubly true for dogs that appeared as if they were nothing more than moochers. Thus, Rags was walking on thin ice and Donovan had to find a way to prove the dog's usefulness to the 7th or be ordered to get rid of him. The way he accomplished this was nothing short of a miracle.

Over the next few weeks Donovan began to note the curious mutt's focus on the act of writing on paper. It was as if he was trying to figure out why this was so important. To capitalize on this interest, Donovan began to jot down meaningless notes, put them into Rags's mouth and jog back to headquarters. As the dog shadowed the man's every step, he always followed. Sensing it was time to take it a step further, the soldier wrote a quick note and placed it into the dog's mouth and pointed toward headquarters. With no other direction, Rags immediately headed off down the road. Within a week Rags had even learned to also bring a note back to Donovan from command.

A few days later, when shellfire took down a communication wire and it was too dangerous to send a human runner back to the artillery headquarters with location information on enemy positions, Donovan wrote a note and gave it to Rags. The dog rushed back to command with the information and American fire was immediately redirected to take out the enemy. From that day forward the 7th Artillery had a messenger that was so small he could move almost unnoticed through enemy fire. Best of all, Rags's focus was so unwavering that he never failed to complete an assignment. Now he was no longer a mascot; he was a soldier.

During the Battle of Laversine, Donovan was given an assignment too dangerous to have Rags with him. On this day a soldier named Welch was given the important task of watching out for the unit's messenger. Welch, a man who deeply missed his own dog back in the States, had for weeks been spoiling Rags with treats. Because of this, Rags treated the soldier with almost as much affection as he did Donovan. Their day together was going well until the Germans redirected their artillery fire. An unexpected wave of shells struck the area where Welch and other members of the 7th were resting. When the first explosion hit, Rags was blown clear and only momentarily dazed, but Welch was badly injured. Rather than running away from danger, as natural instinct demanded, the dog worked his way through a series of tunnels to the incapacitated soldier. When the man didn't move, Rags went into action. Dodging shells, the dog emerged from the trench and raced back to headquarters. Those who greeted him expected a note so when there was none they ignored him. Yet Rags wouldn't give up. He continued to badger the men, tugging at pant legs and yipping until two perplexed soldiers followed him back to Welch. A call for medics was immediately sent out, and with the concerned dog watching, the badly injured man's wounds were treated. The soldier was then transported back to the field hospital.

There is no history about what happened to Welch. With no first name or rank, the man's fate has been lost to history. Legend has it Rags's action saved the man's life, but there is no clear record proving that. What is known is that on that brutal day a dog learned two new skills. The first was being able to identify a wounded man and realize he needed help. The other was understanding who provided that help. The next time a man in the 7th was hit by fire, Rags went directly to a medic. For the remainder of the war the dog would guide dozens of medical crewmen to wounded soldiers.

Rags was not a dog who relished downtime. When Donovan wasn't busy, the mutt grew bored. During these times he would wander around looking for action. On a hot day in late summer the dog jumped out of a trench and in spite of desperate calls urging him to come back, Rags wandered along the Paris-Soissons road into what was known as no-man's-land. With enemy shells falling all around and poisonous gas creeping along the ground, the dog discovered a dead American soldier. Remembering the lesson that every piece of paper was important, Rags noted a folded letter in the fallen man's hand. Pulling it out, he returned the note to Donovan.

A young lieutenant had written this note and given it to the now-dead messenger to take to headquarters. "I have forty-two men, mixed, healthy and wounded. We have advanced to the road but can go no farther. Most of the men are from the 26th Infantry. I am the only officer. Machine guns at our rear, front, right, and left. Send infantry officer to take command. I need machine gun ammunition."

The lieutenant and his men would have died without

Rags sensing a piece of paper was so vital. With the 7th alerted, an artillery barrage was initiated and a rescue unit was sent out. Within an hour the men were saved and Rags was hailed as a hero.

After the Second Battle of the Marne, Donovan was given some time away from the front lines. During those days of rest and relaxation, the soldier made a small gas mask for Rags and finally taught the mutt his first and only trick. When an officer approached, Rags automatically stood on his hind legs and lifted his right front paw over his eyes in a salute. The first man to note the gesture was Major General Charles P. Summerall. The commanding officer of the 1st Division had a reputation of being the most demanding general in Europe and not someone who saw a need for mascot dogs on the front. Yet when he noted Rags saluting, Summerall remarked that perhaps this mutt could teach the whole division something about respect.

With a general's approval, Rags had the run of the camps and took full advantage of his newfound celebrity. In mess halls he quickly learned a few salutes always led to a reward of food and along the streets those salutes brought him praise and plenty of petting. For almost a week he was treated as if he was the king of the hill, but then he had the misfortune of running into a cat. As expected, Rags snapped at the beast before chasing him through the camp and up a tree. The owner of the feline, Colonel Theodore Roosevelt Jr., was not amused even when Rags saluted as he approached. The dog might have been drummed out of service if not for the fact that Donovan's leave was over. Hence, a trip back to the front likely saved Rags's hide.

Once again in the midst of battle, Rags spent most of his days with his muzzle covered by a gas mask. Perhaps this was the reason he grew to depend more upon his ears than his nose. Over the course of that week the dog learned to judge the whistles of incoming artillery shells and somehow sense where they would land. When he realized an explosive was headed his way, he jumped into a trench, fell flat on his belly with legs outstretched, and remained perfectly still. The first time Rags did this the soldiers were confused. The second time they mimicked the dog's response and scrambled into holes for protection. This skill, for which he had not been trained but was instead adapting due to combat, would lead to Rags saving scores of lives over the course of the rest of the war.

The next thing Rags learned through observation made Donovan's job much easier. The soldier spent hours checking phone wires to see which were good and which had been broken or cut. Through observation, Rags somehow realized what his master was doing and began to alert Donovan to which lines were broken even before the man could test them. It seemed the dog could hear the vibration of the wires that were transmitting while also noting the ones that were silent. This unique skill, displayed by no other dog during the war, allowed Donovan to work more efficiently and thus get communication lines back into operation much more quickly. In the end, this also meant Rags was actually a part of changing the course of the war.

One of the dog's most interesting experiences happened when a crew from an observation balloon set down in a meadow where Donovan was working. As the men talked, Rags jumped into the basket and went to sleep. When the sounds of battle suddenly filled the air, the air scouts scrambled back into the balloon and lifted off. They were more than a thousand feet in the air when one of the men noticed the still-sleeping dog.

As the soldiers studied enemy troop movements and identified artillery placements, Rags remained calm. Yet when a German plane emerged from the clouds and began shooting, he began to howl. The men tried to ward off the Fokker with their own guns, but it did little good. On the pilot's second pass the balloon was shredded by fire. One of the men scooped up Rags and crawled over the edge of the basket. After taking a deep breath and glancing down at the ground, he pushed out into the air. A second later he pulled the cord on his parachute. As the canopy opened, the rapid plunge to earth slowed, but the danger grew even more pronounced. The German plane was still firing at the drifting soldiers and their chutes were also drawing ground fire. With bullets passing on every side and Rags barking each time the Fokker grew close, the air scout somehow held on to the dog and made the trip to the ground unharmed. As the man released the harness, Rags hurried across the meadow and back to where he'd last seen his master.

Donovan, who had witnessed the entire episode, urged the dog through a barrage of fire to his side. Reunited, they sought cover.

When the action lessoned, Donovan discovered that the officer in charge of his unit had been killed. Taking command over a handful of tired and scared soldiers, the communication technician led the remaining men to the front where they took part in the battle. This heroic action would pave the way for Donovan to be advanced in rank to sergeant.

In September, with the Germans retreating from St. Michel, the American forces found themselves face-to-face with the enemy. In trenches and on hillsides guns often gave way to hand-to-hand combat. This continued for four days. When Donovan crawled out of trenches to exchange blows with German soldiers, Rags jumped out and chewed at the enemy's hands or feet. The tag team of dog and man resulted in dozens of Germans being killed or taken prisoner and on each occasion Rags and Donovan escaped with only bruises. Donovan was sure it was the distraction created by the dog that saved his life.

During the final American campaign of the war, at the Meuse-Argonne, Donovan was taken out of a combat role and once more put in charge of keeping the communication lines open between the 26th Infantry and 7th Field Artillery. The fighting was fierce and lines were often cut. When the phones went down, Donovan scribbled down messages on enemy positions and Rags raced back through fire to take these important communications to headquarters. One of the notes that got through changed the course of the battle.

> From C.O. 1st Bn. 26th Infantry, Oct. 2 - 12:30 To Captain Thomas, Intelligence Officer: Have artillery that is firing in small, oblong-shaped woods, directly in front and on right of first objective, lengthen range and pound hell out of the woods. Machine gun nests are located there. Legge, Cdg.

Within minutes of Rags's arrival, the nests were knocked out and the men advanced. The dog was then sent back with the message for Donovan to get the phone communications lines restored.

A week later, in the Argonne Forest, a heavy fog filled the air. As the 26th Infantry waited for a German attack, the phone lines went down and lethal mustard gas drifted in the air. Donovan, working on finding a line break, failed to get his gas mask before his lungs filled with the poisonous fumes. Struggling to breathe, he hurriedly scribbled his observations of enemy movements, put a gas mask over Rags's nose and eyes, and gave the mutt the note. He then ordered the dog back to headquarters. Initially Rags was unwilling to leave his badly injured master, but a determined Donovan pushed him out of the trench and into fire. Now running for his life, Rags headed toward the 7th's command position. Dodging bullets, the dog would alternate running as fast as his short legs could carry him and then dropping onto his belly to wait out artillery fire. The journey, though only a few miles, took hours. Rags was almost to command when a fragment from an exploding shell ripped into his foot, ear, and eye. Now blinded in one eye and likely unable to hear, the dog rolled over and limped forward. A second artillery shell exploded several yards to his left again knocking him off his feet. This time when he rose Rags looked dazed. Witnesses described him as slowly wobbling forward a dozen more feet before falling into a trench. A soldier who had anxiously observed the dog's flight for life rushed to his side and found the note. As others gathered, Rags's wounds were treated while Donovan's message was taken to headquarters.

The note gave the 7th not only the information they needed to redirect fire but also a location for Donovan. A medical crew raced to the scene. As they were tending to the soldier's wounds, Donovan asked, "Did my dog make it?" The men didn't have to reply, the sound of redirected American artillery fire gave him the answer. It also meant that hundreds of other soldiers' lives had been saved.

When Donovan arrived at headquarters, he was placed in an ambulance along with Rags. They rode to the hospital together. When told what had happened, the doctors worked on the dog along with the man and even allowed Rags to stay beside the sergeant's cot. This accommodation would be temporary.

Donovan was in such bad shape he was assigned to a hospital ship bound for the United States. As he was loaded into the ambulance, Rags watched. When the truck pulled out, the dog followed. But when Donovan arrived at the ship, the canine was barred from entry. For the next few hours, Rags paced back and forth on the dock crying. The story might have ended there if not for the actions of a wounded colonel who spotted the dog. Knowing that he would not be allowed to carry Rags on board, but also knowing that hundreds if not thousands of lives had been saved by Donovan's "mascot," he picked Rags up, stuffed him under his coat, walked on board, and then hid the dog in his quarters.

There was a strict no-animal policy on the ship. After the ship was a full hour out to sea, a stray cat was found and tossed overboard. Thus, Rags had to remain hidden in order to avoid the same fate. The colonel called all those who knew the dog's story together. Using warlike precision the soldiers worked out a schedule for staying with Rags and devised ways to smuggle him food. When the dog barked, the men did too in order to cover the sounds. The ship's staff came to assume the yelping soldiers were playing some kind of strange game. The band of canine smugglers also bribed medics and nurses attending Donovan to allow Rags visits.

When the ship arrived in Hoboken, New Jersey, the colonel placed Rags into a duffle bag and carried him ashore. When the officer discovered Donovan was being transferred to a hospital at Fort Sheridan in Chicago, the dog was smuggled on the train with the injured communication technician. When they arrived in the Windy City, Rags followed Donovan's ambulance from the train station to the hospital where the staff refused to allow the dog to enter.

For the next few weeks, Rags spent his daylight hours at the hospital's front door and his nights scrounging for food. In a sense, though he was thousands of miles and a lifetime of adventures away from his first days in Paris, his life had come full cycle. He was once again homeless and unwanted.

Just before Christmas, Colonel William N. Bispham observed Rags and wondered why a dog was hanging out at a hospital. He made some calls and discovered the full story of a mutt in France who had saved hundreds of soldiers. On the off chance this might be the canine, he pulled rank and took Rags through the front door and to Donovan's bedside. When the scrawny, hungry dog saw Donovan, his whole demeanor changed. Yipping, he jumped out of Bispham's arms and leaped into the sick man's bed. When Donovan's hand found Rags's small head, the amazed staff cried.

All across the military camp there was talk about a modern Christmas miracle. Though he had no idea as to how the dog had made his way from France to Chicago, Bispham suggested that this was an act of God and the hospital should welcome Rags's daily visits to his master. Doctors, who felt that Donovan's case was all but hopeless, agreed and new protocols were adopted. Bispham also found the dog a place to stay at the base fire station.

For the next few weeks, each morning Rags would leave the fire station, walk to the hospital, and stroll to Donovan's bedside. Each evening, after the base's retreat was

51

played, he returned to the fire station. It was Bispham who accompanied Rags for his final visit with the dying Donovan and it was also Bispham who returned the next day to show the dog the empty bed. Somehow Rags understood what the colonel was trying to explain and never again returned to the hospital. He was now simply the firehouse dog.

A year later Major Raymond W. Hardenberg was transferred to Fort Sheridan. When his two daughters met Rags they brought him home for supper. Within weeks the one-eyed dog was a part of the family. Four years later, when the Hardenbergs were transferred to Governor's Island, New York, Rags was reunited with many of the men the dog had known in France. The press covered the meeting and the dog's fame quickly grew to the point that in 1926 the Long Island Kennel Club honored him for his wartime service. Two years later, as America marked the decade anniversary of the end of World War I, Rags marched with the US Army's 1st Division down the streets of New York. As he had been doing since France, he saluted all the officers he met during that day.

When the 1st Division moved to Washington, DC, Rags went with them. During the last years of his life he remained active, appearing at veteran's reunions and continuing to perk his ears upward whenever someone mentioned Donovan's name. In 1936, when Rags died, most of the nation's newspapers published the story and *The New York Times* included his obituary on a page normally reserved for humans.

Born into a war-stricken environment, growing up homeless and forgotten, discovered and rescued on a day when the French celebrated democracy, the mutt from a Paris alley went on to save thousands of lives before crossing an ocean and half a continent in a gesture of loyalty that will likely never be equaled by man nor dog. In the end it was the salutes of those who served with Rags that spelled out the full meaning that one tiny mutt had on thousands of hardened veterans. He defined love, honor, and service. And, in a very real way, he helped the Allies win a war.

Four

Adoption

It's important to realize that we adopt not because we are rescuers.
No. We adopt because we are rescued.

—David Platt

As Sergeant Leland Leroy "Lee" Duncan carefully made his way across the cratered French landscape the smell of sulfur filled the air. After a year of long days and nights on the often muddy and always heavily mined battlefields, Duncan could almost ignore the putrid odor. But he couldn't dismiss the inhuman nature of this War to End All Wars. In a year, the American had seen enough cruelty and perversion to fill a lifetime of nightmares, and death had been such a frequent visitor that the old Grim Reaper no longer scared him. In fact, they were on a first-name basis.

This was not the way the battle against the Germans has been described in newspapers and at recruiting stations. The war was supposed to be an easy walk in the park for the Americans. Those who encouraged him to volunteer assured Duncan the experience would be little more than a few months camping out with friends coupled with a chance to see Paris. Yet this War to End All Wars was nothing like that. It was death, destruction, cruelty, pain, and suffering all delivered at the same time. It was sleeping in mud and dodging exploding shells. It was making a friend one day and watching him die the next. So the Great War, as the reporters called it, was not great at all. It was terrible and Duncan now believed that if he lived to see peace he would return to the States with nothing but bad memories and visions of death.

Born in Hanford, California, in 1892, Duncan had never had it easy. Deserted by his father and left with a mother who could not provide for him, he spent much of his youth in an orphanage. By the time he was twenty he'd moved to Los Angeles and landed a job at a sporting goods store. Not long after the United States entered what is now known as World War I, Duncan bought into the talk of the glamor of battle, quit his job, and enlisted. He would become one of the first Americans to land on French soil. Wounded in battle, he recovered and became a part of the 135th Air Squadron, where he was assigned to keep the machine guns in top operating condition. He also designed several modifications to the weapons, making them more effective. But on September 15, 1918, while his friends flew, he was delegated to mop-up operations on the always-dangerous French soil.

As they pulled out, an officer warned the sergeant to keep his men on guard. Though it looked clear, there might still be snipers in the area. He and his men had hardly had any sleep over the past few weeks and had eaten little more than slop. They were literally used up. So even as Duncan passed the word to stay focused, he wondered if it would do much good. The unit was simply too worn out to be very alert.

Moving across what had been a German airfield but was now just another plot of ground littered with bomb craters and bodies, Duncan searched the horizon for the enemy. Even though the Germans had retreated, the landscape still showed signs of war's handiwork. Twisted metal and dead horses were on all sides. There were also hundreds of gas masks and thousands of spent shells.

Glancing to his left, Duncan saw a stand of woods. To his right was a group of burned-out buildings surrounded by busted aircraft, and beyond that was an open, flat pasture. It was clear that this had been an airbase only a few days before. It would have to be searched, so the sergeant signaled for a few of his comrades to split off and comb that area.

Scanning the uneven and scarred hillside for mines, Duncan and four of his men slowly made their way to the seemingly deserted German base. A quick examination confirmed the buildings had likely caught on fire after being shelled. The flames then spread to fuel tanks that exploded. As there were no bodies in the destroyed buildings, the base must have been deserted by the time this became the front line. With no signs of life and nothing worth salvaging, Duncan signaled for his group to move forward. Twenty steps later a cry stopped the American in his tracks. Turning his lanky frame back toward the airbase, he pricked his ears and listened. A few seconds later, he heard it again. Somewhere back there, in an area they had somehow missed, an injured man needed their help, and at this moment it didn't matter if he was friend or foe.

Duncan doubted this was a trap, but he also didn't think it wise to take his men with him. As the man in charge he would take the risk. If he was walking into something unexpected there was no use in having several killed for his misjudgment.

Moving forward, his rifle ready, the wary sergeant walked back onto the bombed-out base. He first stopped at the burned barracks. Seeing nothing, he moved on. He was cautiously approaching a wrecked hanger when he once more noted an almost imperceptible cry. There was something or someone not that far away. About a hundred yards from where he stood were the remnants of what looked like a crude chicken coop. A wire fence clinging to what was left of wooden fenceposts surrounded the rickety building, constructed of what appeared to be boards salvaged from a home or barn. One puff of wind would have likely blown the entire thing down.

From his vantage point he spotted no signs of human life. So logic urged Duncan to move on and rejoin his men, but the lure of mystery yanked his heart to the side harder than his mind could pull him forward. Thus, the temptation of finding out what was crying overcame his common sense.

Carefully creeping to his right, his gun locked and ready, Duncan leaned against one of the remaining walls of an aircraft hanger and stared into the makeshift shed. It was deserted. The cries must have been the creaking of rusty hinges on a partially open door.

Satisfied there was nothing to worry about, Duncan walked back toward the field only to be frozen in his tracks by another cry. He was now sure this one was coming from behind the shed.

Retracing his steps, he inched into the area, pushed part of the wire fence down with his rifle butt, and stepped into a section of dirt littered with splintered wood. Now he could hear the cries much more clearly. They seemed to be coming from under a large piece of board just to his left. The four-foot by four-foot panel was probably once a part of the decimated hanger he had looked into a few minutes before. It must have been blown to this spot by a mortar shell.

Bending at the waist, Duncan switched his gun in his right hand while using his left to pick up the nearest corner of the wood. As the sunlight illuminated the hole, he spied five squirming creatures. Covered with dirt, ash, and soot, they appeared to be large rats. As he more closely studied his discovery he realized they were actually puppies. The litter was so young their eyes were still closed. A huge smile crossed his lips: in the midst of war he had found life.

The German retreat had likely come so quickly this group of pups was forgotten. It was also possible their mother had been killed in the artillery assault and the airmen decided it was too much trouble to care for the newborns. The only thing Duncan could really be sure of was that these little ones were hungry.

Setting his gun on the ground, Duncan carefully moved the wood to the side, knelt down, and scooped up one of the pups. As it wiggled in his hand, he stroked its tiny head with his index finger.

"Where's your mother?" Duncan whispered. As the pup yelped in reply the soldier laughed for the first time in weeks. "Yeah, you found a sucker. I'll take care of you all right."

A growl awakened Duncan to the fact he was not alone. Just to his right the mother was lurking, likely having returned from scavenging for food. Though she was not happy her puppies had been found, she was too weak to protest with much more than her voice. Setting the pup down, he pulled off his pack and opened a tin. After giving the hungry dog a few bites of food, he gently petted her head and assured the animal everything was going to be all right. As she happily ate, Duncan turned his attention back to the tiny animal he had recently picked up.

Though he didn't know it then, the tiny, half-dead, German shepherd puppy would dramatically alter the remainder of Duncan's life. Within a few years this refugee, found in the middle of a horrific battle site, would become the most famous dog in the world and would pave the way for Duncan to save thousands of other men in another war that was not yet on the horizon. But that was in the future, for the moment the soldier needed to figure out what he could do to help this mother and her offspring.

As a once-deserted and unwanted child, Duncan felt great empathy for the animals. So he picked up the pups, put them in his backpack, attached a length of rope around the mother dog's neck, and vowed to find a local farm family to take them in. With abject poverty and hunger plaguing most of France, Duncan struck out more than twenty times. During those days his unit spoiled the adoptees. Finally, after more than a month of playing godfather, he convinced one of his commanding officers to take one of the pups, convinced a trio of enlisted men to adopt three more as company mascots, and found a place on a farm for the mother. That left him with a male and female. After a few days dodging enemy bombs that killed others in his unit, Duncan grew convinced the remaining pups were his good luck charms. He christened them—Rintintin and Nénette—popular French dolls modeled after street urchins. Considering where the puppies had been found, the names were appropriate.

In truth, there was no way that the pups should have survived the war. But for the next nine months they managed to dodge bullets, avoid artillery bombardments, and follow their adopted master across hundreds of miles of European battlefields. When Armistice Day was announced and peace finally returned to a region where eleven million military men and another seven million civilians had died, Duncan was faced with a huge problem. Military code strictly prevented all dogs, including those who had served as company mascots, from boarding troop ships back to the United States. Logic told Duncan to find homes for the almost-year-old pups, but they had become as important to him as family. They literally followed him everywhere he went and slept with their muzzles against his body. Thus, using money he had saved as bribes, he managed to smuggle the dogs on board his ship home. By the time they were discovered the ship was well out to sea. And in July 1919, the French-born, German shepherds sailed past the Statue of Liberty and into New York Harbor.

Once in the States, Duncan was assigned to a base in Hempstead, New York, where he found a local breeder who would board Rintintin and Nénette. A few days later, when Duncan got a pass and came to check on his dogs, the kennel owner shared his admiration for the way the pups were trained. Duncan explained he had been forced to teach the pups discipline in order to help them survive in war. He had also taught them tricks to entertain the troops who badly needed a morale boost. The breeder asked Duncan if he would like to learn more about working with dogs. The answer was an immediate yes and over the course of the next few months the sergeant was given a complete education in canine training methods. Yet also during this time tragedy hit him with the force of a bomb. Disease ravaged the kennel, spreading illness that developed into pneumonia from one dog to another. Rintintin and Nénette were among those struck. Using all his scheduled leave, a frantic Duncan hand-fed the dogs and never left their sides. For days both lingered near death, their breathing shallow and their athletic bodies losing mass. In spite of hundreds of prayers and hours of ministering, Nénette died in Duncan's arms, but somehow Rintintin hung on. By the time Duncan's enlistment ended, the dog had beaten the odds and fully recovered.

In late 1919, the dark sable German shepherd and the now-civilian Duncan boarded a train for California. The man went back to working in sporting goods and in his spare time taught his dog, whose name was now spelled Rin Tin Tin, to aid him while hunting. The canine's incredible athletic ability wowed Duncan's friends and they encouraged him to enter the German shepherd in special dog competitions that showcased canine athletic skills. It sounded like a great idea, but that first show proved a disaster. Rin Tin Tin managed to climb and clear a ten-foot wall, but he also threatened every other dog at the show. His growling and snapping at both canines and their handlers caused Duncan to leave in disgrace. To make matters worse, as the pair walked home a delivery truck lost a heavy load of newspapers that fell on top of Rin Tin Tin, breaking his right-front leg. So not only did Duncan lose the contest and have his dog's behavior prove embarrassing, but he was stuck with a huge veterinarian bill and months spent nursing the injured pup back to health.

Almost a year later and after an intense course in proper socialization, Duncan entered a once again healthy Rin Tin Tin in the Los Angeles German shepherd athletic skills show. In the audience was Charley Jones, the inventor of a slow-motion movie camera. To showcase the new invention

Jones had already convinced Babe Ruth to be filmed both hitting and pitching a baseball, but that concept was moved to the back burner when Jones watched Rin Tin Tin win the competition with a jump of almost twelve feet. Timing is said to be everything and when the cameraman convinced Duncan to restage the leap on film it opened the door for a new opportunity for both the dog and his owner.

In 1920 the silent film industry was moving west in search of long sunny days and clear skies. Thus Hollywood, which could claim both, was becoming the center for action pictures. When Rin Tin Tin subbed for a wolf who wouldn't do a stunt in 1922's *The Man from Hell's River*, Duncan made his first few dollars in the motion picture industry. After playing a pet in his next film, Rin Tin Tin caught Jack Warner's eye and within a few weeks Duncan's dog had a starring roll in an action film. In that movie Rin Tin Tin would ride a horse, swim against the tide in a raging river, surf, and bring down a muscular villain. Within a month of the movie's release, Warner Brothers, which had been teetering near bankruptcy, received one thousand letters earmarked for the canine star. Five hit films later, Rin Tin Tin was generating fan mail at the rate of ten thousand letters a week. The dog left to die on a battlefield had become America's newest superstar and in the process saved a studio that would soon become one of the world's most iconic companies.

For the next eight years Duncan's dog was one of the biggest stars in Hollywood. He was such a huge moneymaker that Warner Brothers employed Darryl F. Zanuck to write

Rin Tin Tin's scripts. Nothing was too good for Rin Tin Tin. He was welcomed into the finest hotels and restaurants, rode first class on trains, and was idolized by millions of adults and children all over the globe. While on publicity tours the dog drew thousands to ballparks and arenas. New York City mayor Jimmy Walker even gave the German shepherd the key to the city. Beyond his film roles, Rin Tin Tin was also endorsing everything from collars to dog food. And every film studio in Hollywood was holding casting calls to discover their own dog star.

By the advent of the sound features era in 1928, Duncan had moved his family and the canine hero into one of the city's nicest neighborhoods. Tour buses came by daily as eager fans hoped to get a look at one of the world's big stars. More often than not they left disappointed as Rin Tin Tin was usually at the studio or on location. Acting with some of Hollywood's greatest names, such as Myrna Loy, Noah Beery, John Barrymore, and Lupe Velez, the dog starred in more than a dozen full-length talking, or in this case barking, films in just two years. In 1929 the studio created a series of B movies, aimed at families and children called the *Rin Tin Tin Thrillers* that proved the canine actor could pack audiences into theaters even without big-time costars. Even as he aged the dog remained at the top of this game. Yet change was on the horizon.

As talking movies grew more sophisticated, Rin Tin Tin's impact on Hollywood took a nosedive. By 1931, most of the studios had turned their backs on animal films. A year later, the dog trainer's home was destroyed by fire. In the blaze he lost all he held dear except for his family and Rin Tin Tin. A few months later, as he was building a new home on Club View Drive, a bank failure resulted in Duncan losing his investments. About this same time a fourteen-year-old Rin Tin Tin was deemed too old to perform and was cut loose by Warner Brothers.

Once a star's light flickered out or times and tastes changed, Hollywood and the executives who ran the studio didn't hesitate to move on. Along with Rin Tin Tin a host of silent movie icons were now out of work and all but forgotten. As Duncan struggled to pay bills and fan mail trickled to just a letter or two a week, it seemed the aging former dog star had only one true friend. Almost every night after she finished working at MGM, the world's newest and most celebrated female sensation, Jean Harlow, walked over from her home to Duncan's to bring Rin Tin Tin a treat. For several minutes the blonde bombshell, as she was now known, would rub the graying dog's head. If Rin Tin Tin was going to have one fan remember him, the animal-loving Harlow seemed to be the perfect choice.

On August 10, 1932, just before noon, Duncan noticed his dog struggling to stand. Once on his feet, Rin Tin Tin staggered for a few moments and then pitched forward. He would never rise again. A half an hour later the family vet examined the aging star and determined the dog had suffered a stroke. The medical professional sadly informed Duncan that Rin Tin Tin would be dead within minutes. As the dog lingered in the home's living room, Duncan stayed by his side and waited for the inevitable. Fifteen minutes passed, then an hour, and Rin Tin Tin continued to fight. As the dog's breathing grew more shallow, the trainer begged his struggling canine friend to let go, but the dog who had played a hero so many times just kept breathing.

Eight hours past the time the vet assured Duncan that Rin Tin Tin would pass, there was a knock on the home's front door. Sweeping into the room, her eyes filled with tears, was Jean Harlow. When alerted to what happened, the beautiful blonde had rushed to see the fallen dog as soon as she finished filming. When she spoke, somehow Rin Tin Tin found the strength to wag his tail. Harlow fell to the floor, placed the German shepherd's head in her lap, and whispered what millions of fans would have said just a few years before. "I love you, Rinty." The dog died just moments later.

The studio might have believed that no one wanted the dog star anymore, but when word spread in the Hollywood community of Rin Tin Tin's passing, the town went into mourning unseen since the death of Rudolph Valentino. Across the nation radio stations interrupted programming with the news. Newspapers around the globe even printed his obituary and as they read those words millions cried as if they had lost a family member. But as a mournful and despondent Duncan buried Rin Tin Tin in the backyard, he was still convinced that when the dog died his career and influence had died with him. He knew that within months the bank would foreclose on his home and he and his family would be on the streets looking for work. But just as a world war had brought Duncan to Rin Tin Tin, another world event would save him.

In 1933, the Chicago World's Fair booked Duncan and his new dog, Rin Tin Tin II, nicknamed Rinty, as an attraction. With crowds flocking to the Windy City, the son of the world's most famous dog had the chance to charm hundreds of thousands. The press and acclaim created by the live performances made its way back to Hollywood. A small independent studio, Mascot, sensed potential and signed the second-generation dog to a contract. Seven years and fourteen films later, his future secured by investments and savings, Duncan and his dog were on top of the world. Yet growing tired of the motion-picture grind and the fickle nature of Hollywood, Duncan retired, bought a ranch, and moved to the country.

Even as fans focused their attention on other stars and the movie studios decided once again they no longer needed dog actors, there was an organization where the original Rin Tin Tin's exploits were still being studied. And in late 1941, just after the United States entered World War II, the US Army sent a delegation to Rancho Rin Tin Tin to talk to Lee Duncan. Amazed by the stunts they had witnessed in the now-all-but-forgotten silent films, the military wanted to pick the trainer's brain in order to design and develop a program that could train dogs for action in combat. The irony of finding an orphan dog in the midst of war and having that dog inspire the army to employ dogs in this new war was not lost on Duncan. In fact, it prompted him to ask to return to active duty and bring the second generation of Rin Tin Tin with him. For the next four years Duncan would choose and train hundreds of dogs that saw duty in the Second World War.

The canines Duncan trained, as well as what military trainers learned from Duncan and Rinty, would save countless lives during World War II. The skills once used on movie sets would be employed in war to deliver messages, medicines, and supplies and fend off enemies in hand-to-hand combat. During the four years of war Duncan's trained dogs would toss themselves on grenades, drag injured men out of the line of fire, and comfort dying soldiers on the battlefield. They would also become companions that offered love during lulls in battle. One of those, Rin Tin Tin III, would return from Europe a decorated war hero.

When World War II ended, Duncan and the third generation, Rin Tin Tin III, returned to Hollywood. After several films he found his greatest success on television. For five years, this current generation's Rin Tin Tin actually played a military dog in one of ABC's most beloved series. Yet in spite of all the acclaim he won on television Lee Duncan always believed the best moments of his life were his time spent helping the US military train dogs as soldiers. And each time he received a letter from a man whose life had been saved by a dog, Duncan grew more sure that his rescuing a puppy during World War I was not just the most important act of his life, but in thousands of other lives too.

FIVE

SECOND CHANCE

We all have big changes in our lives that are more or less a second chance.

—Harrison Ford

Except for those who work in aviation, Gander, Newfoundland, is an unfamiliar place. In truth, most people have never even heard of this Canadian city of just under twelve thousand. Yet Gander was one of the most important strategic points in the world during World War II and has remained a vital hub for aviation ever since. In large part the city owes its existence to Hitler's rise to power in Germany as does the heroic dog that shares the city's name.

When the Great War ended in 1918, everyone figured the world had learned a lesson. Yet within a decade and a half, historians and politicians were discussing the possibility of a second world war. These concerns grew as they witnessed Nazi Germany's massive arms build up and Imperial Japan seeking to enlarge its military, political, and economic influence in Asia. Even though the League of Nations was preaching peace, by the mid-1930s the fear of another global conflict had pushed scores of countries to increase military spending and devote more resources to new technologies. America's northern neighbor was one of those looking with apprehension toward the future. Though thousands of miles away from Germany and Japan, and seemingly protected by two vast oceans, Canada only had to study the skies to understand the world was now a much smaller place. The Great War had transformed the airplane from novelty to a machine of death and most foresaw airpower as being the key to winning the next war. It was that kind of thinking that literally put Gander on the map.

In 1935 a foreboding patch of ground in Newfoundland suddenly saw a small group of uniformed tourists. Until this time, except for hearty bands of fishermen, this part of Canada had never been a destination point. Yet as it was at the most northern and eastern part of North America, the Canadian military was ready to give the island a second look. Their study found that in the age of aviation Newfoundland could literally be transformed into a "gas station." By creating a major air base on the island, planes traveling from England to the United States or from the United States and Canada to Europe would have a place to refuel.

Once the budget was approved, families from all across Canada moved to wooded, windswept Newfoundland to help accomplish the monumental task of constructing the new air facility. In one of the most obscure spots on the globe a modern city would arise. The street signs echoed

Canada's new and robust passion for aviation. New residents lived and worked on thoroughfares named for the likes of Earhart, Lindbergh, and Rickenbacker. And when the locals picked a name for this new community, they also looked upward to a bird that had been flying the Canadian skies for thousands of years: the gander.

In a place where the weather was often unforgiving, the scope of the Gander project was huge. Starting with nothing, the Canadian military created a base equal with any other on the face of the globe. Along with hangars, runways, control towers, and barracks for the airport, homes, stores, and motion picture theaters popped up. Through teamwork and grit the impossible was accomplished, and after three years of construction, Captain Douglas Fraser made the first landing at what was then called the Newfoundland Airport. The celebration that day in 1938 included toasts, speeches, and a dance. Yet within a week, as the skies filled with aircraft, watching planes land no longer created a stir. And over the next seven years, as a refueling site for Canadian, British, and American bombers hopping across the Atlantic, Gander's runways would see more than twenty thousand planes land and take off.

When the British declared war on Germany in 1939, Canada quickly joined the fight. As the conflict in Europe and Africa heated up, construction at Gander increased exponentially and even more people moved to the island to fill the needs created by this massive military buildup. One of these new families would unknowingly lay a cornerstone for history and set in motion the creation of a legend by simply choosing a dog completely unsuited for their needs.

Newfoundlands are like the St. Bernards of Canada. Weighing 150 pounds, with massive heads, thick necks, and shaggy coats, the web-footed breed was developed in the 1600s by fishermen who lived and worked on the island. Sharing an ancestral line with the ancient mastiff, the breed pulled carts, served as canine pack mules, guarded boats, helped in dragging fish-filled nets and, because of their unparalleled ability as swimmers, were even trained for water rescues. Countless stories recount the tales of fishermen who fell overboard and were saved by Newfoundlands that fearlessly leaped into the ocean to drag drowning men back to their boats. Thus, on the windswept island, the breed was the stuff of legends.

Newfoundland dogs also came to represent the personality of the island's residents. The people who called this often-foreboding place home were robust, outgoing, and fearless. They prided themselves in their ability to survive the Arctic winters and thrive in the stormy summers. When not at work, Newfoundlanders were playful and fun loving. The men who called this spot home were also known for being intensely loyal to those they considered family. And the breed named for Newfoundland mirrored all of those traits. Their courage and fortitude were so revered and their stamina so great that Lewis and Clark purchased a Newfoundland to accompany them on their exploration of the Louisiana Purchase.

As young, healthy men entered the military after the outbreak of war, many fishermen gave up the sea and moved to Gander to fill empty construction jobs. While they might have left their boats and nets behind, the fishermen brought along their good-natured, outgoing dogs. By 1940, when a family named Hayden moved to Gander, Newfoundlands had become fixtures in the city. So it was hardly surprising when Mr. Hayden started looking for a pet that would protect his home and serve as a companion to his young children that a retired fisherman convinced the father he couldn't go wrong with a Newfoundland. A deal was made, and a puppy purchased and brought home. For a while the dog named Pal seemed a perfect fit.

The pup, then about the size of a spaniel, spent hours tagging along Gander's streets with the children. He chased balls, ran after bicycles, and slept in the children's room. As he quickly grew, the kids rigged a small sleigh for Pal to pull and he would merrily take them for rides along the city streets. In the summers the Newfoundland became a part of rugby and baseball games, though he didn't play by the rules. Pal would look for opportunities to steal a bounding ball and race off with it, forcing the children to chase him down. During these days, a time when more and more Canadians were going overseas to battle the Nazis and the toll of that fighting offered little good news, Pal's antics served as a wonderful diversion for the Hayden children and all who watched the energetic, growing pup. Yet just like storms often come without warning in

Newfoundland, unseen trouble was brewing for the family and its pet.

Intelligent dogs need responsibilities and focus and Pal had neither. His rambunctious nature, lack of formal training, and size were a formula that led to his undoing. Not only was Pal soon eating the Haydens out of house and home, he was also constantly getting into trouble. Mischief from a puppy was cute but when a 150-pound dog pulled a clothesline to the ground, chased cats, scattered trash, played tag with postmen, or cleared a table with its wagging tail, things got ugly.

For a while the Haydens' love of their pet overruled common sense. While they dreaded the phone call complaining about Pal, they had grown so devoted to the shaggy behemoth they constantly forgave him for his increasingly uncivilized behavior. When the dog knocked a six-year-old girl to the ground, inflicting a deep scratch on her face, Pal's standing as the community's canine clown dramatically changed. Because the wound required medical treatment, the city was notified and Pal was put on a very short leash. The family was told they had to either find Pal a new home or move out of town. If they didn't, the dog, now designated a dangerous menace, would be put down.

Frantically the Haydens searched for a way to save their misunderstood canine. But while many thought the powerful and bumbling dog was cute, no one wanted to adopt an eating machine. With the clock ticking the Haydens called the Canadian Air Force hoping the local base could train Pal as a guard dog. The military's rejection seemed to guarantee the Newfoundland a one-way ticket to the death house.

With impatient local authorities demanding Pal be given to them, the Haydens continued to look for someone who could offer the Newfoundland a second chance. The big dog was close to eating his final meal when a member of the 1st Battalion of Royal Rifles heard his story. The soldier convinced his friends a dog would be a welcome addition to their unit. In 1940, just days before he was to be put down, Pal moved into the barracks and was given a new name: Gander. In a humorous ceremony, a collar with sergeant stripes was placed around the canine's thick neck.

The 1st Battalion of Royal Rifles was made up of two thousand men from Quebec. Because they were away from home, Gander offered these soldiers a chance to revisit their innocent boyhoods. With only fun in mind, they weren't interested in training the dog for military service but rather enjoyed a companion that was as rowdy as they were. So Gander's behavior changed little. Like the men who had adopted him as their mascot, he played rough, partied hard, and created endless havoc. As a part of his routine, Gander raided the base's trashcans, barked during roll calls, and took every opportunity to sleep on freshly pressed uniforms. He was everything a military dog shouldn't be and the men of the 1st encouraged Gander to stay that way.

By the late summer of 1941, the 1st Battalion of Royal Rifles were aware combat was in their near future, but they didn't know where they would be headed. The most likely destination seemed to be Africa where they would be fighting the Nazis in desert sands, so they were somewhat shocked when told to pack for a trip to Hong Kong. At this time, Axis powers had shown no interest in the island city, so the British colony was still a destination point for tourists. Rather than a military mission, to those of the 1st this seemed like a Christmas wish come true. In October 1941, after receiving their final orders, the men from Quebec left Newfoundland for Asia taking their mascot along for the ride.

In the midst of war Hong Kong was an oasis of peace and tranquility. When not on duty at the garrison, the men of 1st hit the town, spent their money at the nightspots, danced until dawn, got to know the locals, and often woke up with hangovers. Their mascot had a pretty good life too.

Though he suffered in the heat, Gander was actually treated better in Hong Kong than he had been in Canada. That was due in large part to the fact that members of the 1st Battalion of Royal Rifles had money in their pockets and time on their hands and merchants wanted to get a piece of that action. If business owners spoiled the dog then the men spent more cash. Thus Gander quickly grew fond of the local food and lapping beer from a bowl. Gander spent mornings sleeping on a veranda and afternoons under shade trees. To help the dog deal with the unrelenting heat and humidity, the soldiers even convinced local hotels to allow Gander to use the swimming pools. The huge canine also became a frequent visitor to Hong Kong's many fountains.

The party atmosphere wouldn't go on forever. Newspaper headlines screamed the bad news from Europe and the fine print hinted at potential Japanese aggression in Hong Kong. Only a few months before in Canada, the clock had been ticking for Gander, and his future seemed uncertain. In early December in Asia, if one listened closely, that clock could be heard again but this time it was counting down the minutes for an entire city.

On December 8, 1941, just hours after Japan hit Pearl Harbor, the Japanese military stormed the beaches of Hong Kong. With little warning almost two thousand Canadian men and their mascot experienced war firsthand, and it was not a fair fight.

The forces defending Hong Kong were outnumbered four to one and after the initial attack, government and military officials realized the city would soon be lost. The five British planes assigned to the garrison were quickly destroyed and, except for raids by American pilots flying for the Chinese Air Force, there was no relief from the Japanese assault. Hiding behind rocks that overlooked the beaches, in ditches along roads, and on tree-covered hills, British, Indian, and Canadian forces did everything in their power to hold their ground, but the overpowering Japanese war machine was relentless as it patiently marched forward. For days the battle raged both day and night and the exhausted 1st Battalion of Royal Rifles was asked to dig deeper and fight harder and encouraged to conserve ammunition, food, and medicine. The enlisted men had to look no further than the eyes of the officers to understand their fate. There would be no victory; they were fighting for time and pride.

The big black Newfoundland might have never been trained for military service, but Gander proved a quick study. He noted the destructive power of bombs and grenades and ran from them. He quickly grasped who was shooting at his friends and learned to seek cover during heavy assaults. He also was soon able to identify the direction from which the Japanese were mounting their attacks and warn the men of the 1st before the attacks began. By the second week of the war Gander decided that trying to stay out of harm's way behind Canadian lines was simply not enough. On a night as black as pitch the dog noted a small group of Japanese soldiers circling behind the twenty men he was with. When rifleman Reginald Law heard Gander growl, he attempted to keep Gander quiet in order not to give away the unit's position. The dog ignored Law, barked, and charged from cover, and a few seconds later the Canadian heard a scream. Peeking over a rock brought a smile to the exhausted and demoralized Law's face. Gander had sunk his teeth into one of the enemy's legs. With the dog holding the Japanese soldier in place, several more enemy soldiers appeared in an effort to help their comrade. With the Japanese group's position revealed, the soldiers from the 1st Battalion of Royal Rifles had little problem picking off the invaders. The Japanese soldiers who somehow escaped the hail of fire were chased more than a hundred yards by the angry black dog.

Gander's first taste of combat offered much-needed

inspiration to the outmanned Canadians. As the dog returned from running off the small Japanese invading party, he was greeted with hugs, pats on the head, and a few treats fished from backpacks. Yet while this moment offered something to celebrate, there was still no escaping the earsplitting sounds of rifles or the screams of dying men. By the moment, the war was growing even more intense.

Japanese ships began raining terror from the skies and huge shells fell and exploded all around the littered landscape. With each passing moment more Japanese soldiers were hitting the beaches and storming toward the garrison. The odds that had always been against the Canadians were now overwhelming. So while Gander might have turned the tide for a moment, thus saving twenty men with his mad charge into the night, the end result would remain the same. The Japanese were going to win.

Over the next few weeks, the men of the 1st Battalion of Royal Rifles had a chance to defend their positions in the daytime. When they could see the enemy, they were able to hold their ground. But at night they were all but helpless. Employing the cover of darkness the Japanese silently made their way through the brush to within feet of Canadian positions. More often than not, Gander was the only one that could sense their presence. Much like he had during his days of playing rugby and baseball with neighborhood children, he would launch himself over boulders or between trees and tackle enemy soldiers. The Newfoundland's actions alerted the Canadians to the direction of the attack and kept them from being surprised. As word of Gander's abilities and courage spread, other combat groups asked to borrow him but to no avail. Law and his friends now felt the Newfoundland offered them the only chance at perhaps beating the odds and surviving the battle for Hong Kong.

During lulls in the fighting, as men rested and ate, they began to total the times Gander had saved their lives by repelling attacks. Their stories quickly spelled out something remarkable. The dog had likely been as responsible as any man in delaying Japanese victory. When soldiers hurriedly scribbled letters to loved ones, they described the mighty dog pinning enemy soldiers to the ground or chasing after them as they retreated screaming through the underbrush. Now they didn't write of the canine as a mascot as they had before the war, but they gave him almost human qualities. He was their friend, comrade, and brother. They owed him their lives. Thus, in their minds, Gander had more than earned his rank of sergeant, with some suggesting he be given a battlefield promotion.

As the battle for Hong Kong dragged on, the Canadians were forced to give ground. Under hails of bristling fire, scores of men died during the retreats. During one of those backward sprints, one member of the 1st Battalion of Royal Rifles screamed, falling from his position out into the open road. Writhing in pain, he tried to crawl back to cover, but couldn't find the strength. As he yelled for help, a half dozen Japanese soldiers, their guns drawn, raced forward. Just as the Canadians turned to fire, Gander exploded from a hiding place in the brush and rushed the enemy. The half a dozen shocked Japanese infantrymen turned their attention from the injured Canadian and aimed their weapons at the dog. As rapid bursts of fire rang out, the determined Gander kept coming. Growling, snapping, and yelping, the Newfoundland tackled the Japanese soldier nearest the fallen Canadian soldier. Only by using his rifle as a club did the soldier manage to free himself from the dog's grip and race from the scene. With fear and panic written on their faces, the soldier's comrades turned tail and ran as well. This time the dog didn't chase, rather he stood over the injured Canadian as if to shield him from further harm.

Coming out of the brush, members of the 1st picked up their wounded friend. As they carried him to safety, Gander defiantly stood in the middle of the road and barked. It seemed he was demanding those who had injured his friend return to finish the fight.

By December 18 there was little question as to the outcome of the battle for Hong Kong. Though they had fought hard for ten days, the Allies would soon fall. With their supplies dwindling and surviving on little more than grit, the Canadians and Brits held on hoping against hope the Japanese would slow their assault long enough for Allied or Chinese reinforcements to come to the garrison's aid. It was not to be.

By now every member of the 1st Battalion of Royal Rifles had experienced death in some way. Hundreds had been killed and those who remained alive had taken an enemy's life. The men were naturally numb, exhausted, hungry, and confused. As they waited for the invaders' next wave, seven weary Canadians sat behind rocks and took turns petting the dog that had become so much more than a mascot. Just after midnight, in a place called Ley Mun, talk turned to Gander's seeming superpower. The dog had raced through enemy fire a hundred times and never been hit. He'd taken down men armed with knives and bayonets and never been bloodied. Artillery shells had landed within yards of the black beast and he had not absorbed any shrapnel. And as the men shared their meager rations with the huge animal, one asked for a roll call of those who felt Gander had saved their lives. The vote was unanimous.

A few minutes later, just after midnight, the lull ended as a large group of Japanese crawled through the brush toward their position. Suddenly the air was again filled with lead and the weary Canadians were forced to once more grab their weapons and reenter the war. The enemy assault group quickly surrounded the seven members of the 1st. With no clear path for retreat, the men were pinned down in an area the size of a handball court.

With gunfire coming from every direction and the well-hidden enemy now less than thirty feet away, the Canadians said final prayers and scanned the darkness for anything that was moving. Less than five minutes after the assault began, a grenade landed in the middle of their position. As fourteen eyes studied the fist-sized explosive, time slowed to a crawl. There was nowhere to run and now no time to live. Knowing they were an instant from death, the horrific sounds of battle were muted by thoughts of loved ones back home, favorite foods, and special songs. And except for one sergeant, no one moved.

In his ten days of combat, Gander had learned of the destructive power of a grenade. He'd seen the weapon blow men apart. The big dog's instincts and experience had to be demanding he run and seek cover. Yet rather than move farther from the grenade, as if possessed, he leaped forward, picked up the hand-tossed explosive like a tennis ball, turned, and charged toward the enemy's position. The big Newfoundland made it a half a dozen steps before the weapon exploded, killing him instantly.

The seven whose lives Gander saved were soon captured. Yet rather than being taken to a stockade created as a temporary prisoner-of-war camp, the men were rushed to Japanese command headquarters. During intense one-on-one interrogations, enemy officers peppered them with only a few questions about troop strengths and weapons, while the main thrust of the interviews centered on "black beasts." Japanese intelligence wanted to know how many demonic creatures the Allies had in their force and how the monsters were trained as lethal weapons of war.

On Christmas Day the Allies surrendered. The officers who met with the enemy leaders were also peppered with the same questions as the men captured a week before. The Japanese demanded to know what kind of animal the Brits and Canadians were using and why gunfire had no effect on it. Sensing an opportunity to pedal false intelligence, the word was passed for prisoners to inflate their story of the "black devil" or "black beast." Thus, for the next four years the story of the "black beast" grew on a daily basis.

After the war, those who survived near starvation and squalor in the prisoner camps shared stories of how Gander had not just saved many of their lives during the first ten days of the battle for Hong Kong but also brought them hope with his antics during their long days of captivity. Many still felt his presence in their midst and began to believe that Gander was always with them in spirit.

More than six decades after the war ended, a Hong Kong Veterans Memorial Wall was dedicated in Ottawa. Chiseled into stone were the names of 1,977 Canadians who participated in that battle. At the bottom of that list is Sergeant Gander.

The city of Gander exists in large part because of war. On land that no one wanted, an airbase was created as a defense against those who would inflect senseless evil on others. Yet in military lore the Gander that strikes up a sense of awe is not as much a place as a dog that the city officials of Gander felt was a nuisance. Thanks to a last-minute lifeline tossed out by a group of soldiers, the black canine escaped death row. And less than a year later, though not trained for combat, Sergeant Gander would knowingly lay down his life for those who had given him a second chance to live. To many, Gander remained the best symbol of the courage, nature, and spirit that defines Newfoundland.

Six

Resistance

The history of liberty is a history of resistance.
　　　　　　　　　　　　　　　—Woodrow Wilson

During World War II, a Chinese-born English Pointer proved that the love of an animal can inspire sick, starving men to defy all conceivable odds and survive brutal, inhumane treatment, disease, starvation, and loss of freedom. Yet for this dog, Judy, to move from a riverboat mascot to the only official canine prisoner of war would require a remarkable cast of heroes, a long parade of seemingly improbable events, and an almost demonic series of villains who were bent on victory at any cost.

In the late winter of 1936, in a small private kennel in Shanghai, China, a litter of purebred English Pointer puppies was born. Though all were healthy, one proved especially active and intelligent. She was also sneaky, crafty, and a bit belligerent. She was at that moment a rebel without a cause, but in time she would be given a motive for rebellion and use it wisely.

When the energetic pup was two months old she was a master at digging out of pens, opening doors, ignoring her owner's calls, and racing through the streets of a city teeming with life and danger. Though war had yet to be declared, Shanghai, with its convergence of cultures, was ready to erupt. The city was a crown jewel of the British Empire, but it was also coveted by both China and Japan. Due to its strategic location it is not surprising that long before World War II the Japanese were making plans to create a base of operations in Shanghai.

Even in the best of times Shanghai was a dangerous place for a roaming dog. It was teeming with people, cars, carts, and oxen. On top of that, canines were seen as a food source by thousands who lived in the city. Thus, many strays were captured, butchered, and placed on menus in restaurants and homes. During one of her escapes, Judy might have been headed toward that same fate when she confronted Japanese soldiers bullying a local shopkeeper. As the elderly business owner absorbed a series of blows from the visitors, the pup flew into action tearing at the soldier's pants cuffs. A few kicks only stoked her passion for the fight. But while she was game, she was also smart, and when the battle grew dangerous, she found a hiding place. A few days later she also found her way back to the kennel.

Due to her roaming nature it is doubtful Judy would have lived a very long life if the crew of the British gunboat *Gnat* had not been looking for a mascot. By seagoing standards, the *Gnat* was a small vessel, just over two hundred feet long. It was rusty, out of date, and home for a crew of about fifty. Now more than twenty years old, it was used mainly for river patrols. And while all the other British vessels in Shanghai had mascots, the *Gnat* didn't.

On a late summer day the men of the "insect class" boat fanned out across the city looking for any breathing thing they could adopt as a symbol. Standards dictated the mascot needed to define the crew's attitude as well as the *Gnat's* mission. Other ships were already using monkeys, parrots, cats, and goats. So the *Gnat's* crew turned their focus to dogs and began to visit kennels. Of all the canines they saw, the white-and-liver-brown Judy stood out as being both regal and different. In fact, the men liked her for the same reason the kennel owner wanted to get rid of her: she had an attitude! Besides, no ship had a hunting dog that pointed when prey was spotted, which was precisely the *Gnat's* job: to find and point out the enemy. So a deal was made, Judy was placed on a leash, and the team triumphantly led the pup back to the harbor. Though money had changed hands, in truth the kennel owner might have given the dog away because of the grief she caused him with her constant escapes. And while the kennel proprietor didn't need or likely want a canine with those skills, a few years down the road men in another place would.

The crew opted to give the dog a proper English name and title: Judy of Sussex. They also assigned seaman Jan "Tankey" Cooper the task of taking care of the new mascot. While Tankey would feed her, address her needs, and attempt to teach her the basic obedience skills needed for shipboard life, he would never really own her. It would be years before any one person could claim Judy's heart.

In November the *Gnat* pulled out of the harbor to patrol the Yangtze River. The crew's job was to keep an eye on the Japanese Imperial forces, the Chinese military, a growing body of Chinese communist rebels, and pirates. While the crew was not worried about actually taking fire from the Chinese and Japanese, they quickly discovered the pirates were combative and lethal.

A perceptive Judy learned to recognize the sounds of pirate vessels. When she heard the sound, she went into hunter mode—standing perfectly still and pointing in the direction of the potential attackers. For the first time she became more than a mascot; she had developed a skill. When Judy went rigid the seamen got ready for action.

For a few months the river thieves were the thrust of the *Gnat's* mission. Time and time again they would face off against the overmatched pirates, subdue them, put them out of operation, and move on. Yet the pirates were about to become the least of Judy and the crew's problems.

As the months passed the Brits began to witness more confrontations between the Chinese and Japanese. In late 1936 these games of chicken escalated to armed conflict. By the spring of 1937 the waters were red with blood as Imperial Japan declared war on China. With a ferocity not seen since the Great War (World War I), the Asian powers opened up what, in time, would grow to become a part of World War

II. For the moment, the British were the observers, but that would not last long. As the powerful Japanese war machine chewed up the outmanned Chinese forces, the island nation began to test the English resolve.

Over the course of the next two years Judy learned to mistrust the Japanese as much as she did the pirates. Though not at war with the British, the Japanese found excuses to steer their ships dangerously close to the aging English vessel. With each threatening act, Judy grew rigid and ready for action. During those tense moments the crew came to realize that if their lives ever were on the line, the dog would jump right into the fray.

When not on duty, Judy the adult dog was very much the same as Judy the puppy. She grew bored and found ways to get in trouble. When the ship was docked, she would sneak off the deck and roam the streets. Local merchants and farmers drove her off the property and cats gave her a wide berth. There were times when her rambling junkets would turn into hours of exploring, but when she heard the ship's bell she always hurried back to join her crew. She understood her place and loved her position.

Though initially assigned a doghouse on the rear deck, Judy so quickly endeared herself to the *Gnat*'s crew she was given the run of the ship. She had a place in the galley where she ate, toys that littered all areas of the vessel, and a bed in the officers' quarters. Her original crew spoiled her rotten and when a new group of seamen replaced them in 1938, the royal treatment continued. Judy might not have known how to salute or do any impressive tricks, but the white-and-liver-spotted hound had enough personality to win over even a skeptic.

Judy was three when the *Gnat* was junked and the crew was given a new gunboat: the HMS *Grasshopper*. As this vessel had the potential for both river and open sea work, the Pointer expanded her horizons. She not only now pointed out possible hostile vessels before they came into sight, but she grew to distinguish the differences in the engine sounds of the British aircraft and those of Imperial Japan. Thus, Judy became the *Grasshopper*'s best plane spotter.

The world dramatically changed on December 8, 1941, when the Japanese declared war on England and invaded Singapore. No longer were the members of the crew spectators; they were active participants in a life-and-death struggle for world dominance. The enemy had been defined and Judy's barks, pointing muzzle, and rigid tail gave gunners a heads-up on the direction from which lethal aircraft were approaching.

For the *Grasshopper* and its crew, the first weeks of the war were nerve-racking and disheartening. In the Pacific the British were outmanned and there wasn't enough time to get reinforcements in place to hold the Crown's territory in Southeast Asia. As their bases began to be overrun, the *Grasshopper*'s crew knew the odds of ever seeing England again were growing longer. Still, for two months they continued to hold their ground and inflict some damage. Yet, on February 13, it was time to admit defeat and retreat.

Receiving orders to evacuate British subjects, including scores of women and children, the gunboat took hundreds of civilians on board and set course for Australia.

In these tense times, Judy became the *Grasshopper*'s personal greeter and babysitter. She happily welcomed the hundreds of adults who fled to the boat in hopes of escaping the Japanese. She also played her part in keeping excited children occupied on the overflowing decks.

Not long after the *Grasshopper* was steaming across the sea, Judy made her way back to the bow. With only the open ocean on all sides, she turned her gaze to the skies. Even though no human had spotted them, Judy seemed sure Japanese planes were just over the horizon. When she tensed and pointed, the crew realized the war was about to visit them once more. A few minutes later the sky was filled with enemy aircraft.

The men of the *Grasshopper* fought hard but they were simply outmanned. As Judy barked and the crew battled, bombs fell and the ship's decks were littered with machine-gun fire. In just a few minutes the ship took several direct hits. Knowing his badly injured vessel was doomed, the captain steered the boat toward an uncharted island in the Dutch East Indies. Running at full bore, he beached the *Grasshopper* and ordered the crew to evacuate the civilians. For several hours lifeboats ferried civilians and military personnel to the beach. While the Japanese planes were now gone, having moved on to other targets, prospects for survival, even without enemy fire, seemed long. The island offered few food sources and apparently had no fresh water. So desperate was the situation that only hours after landing did the crew realize Judy was not on the island. Most figured the dog had drowned while trying to swim to shore or had been badly injured and died on the ship. Yet, with the situation so desperate, there was no time to mourn.

As the seamen and civilians dug in, the ship's officers met to discuss their limited options. Without water and very little food, they had at most a week. But while the *Grasshopper* was too damaged to fix and refloat, the fires had somehow gone out without completely consuming the vessel. Thus, there was a chance there was still food and water on the gunboat. So the best option was sending a team back to the ship and scavenging anything they could find. After paddling a dingy out to the *Grasshopper*, the salvage party discovered one member of their crew still standing watch over British property. A very much alive Judy greeted the men with a happy bark and a wagging tail. A half an hour later her paws were back on firm ground.

On Shipwreck Island, a small crew of trained marines who had evacuated along with the civilians used every tool at their disposal to find sources of fresh water but came up empty. As the exhausted and demoralized team rested, one of them observed Judy put her nose to the ground as if she was hunting. After several minutes she finally stopped along the beach and barked. When no one came forward to see why she was so upset, Judy began to dig. The curious marines finally rose and wandered over to the place where the dog had removed a couple of feet of sand. They were shocked to see her lapping water from the bottom of the hole. A quick test proved it was fresh. Judy had somehow done what the trained men could not and in the process bought the hundreds trapped on the island some precious time.

Even with a source of water the days on the island would not be pleasant. The military personnel created a makeshift camp and tried to maintain some sense of order, but the civilians were completely unprepared for what they were facing. The weather was hot and humid, the island was home to poisonous insects and snakes, and food was scarce. One long day drifted into another and no ships were spotted on the horizon. On the fifth day after the battle, as morale sank even lower, an ancient trading boat pushed past the *Grasshopper*'s remains. Sailing under a Dutch flag, the crew of the ship set anchor and welcomed the refugees aboard. Once the hundreds of survivors were secure, they were taken to the island of Singkep.

For the moment Singkep was under Dutch control, but everyone knew a Japanese invasion would surely happen in the next few days. With no other choice, the Brits, including the civilian women and children, secured a boat and pushed up a river through the jungle. This water route soon proved impassible and, with Judy leading the way, the crew was forced to cut trails through the dense jungle. Along the way they battled crocodiles, snakes, and leeches. Weeks later, exhausted and sick, they finally reached Padang where they hoped to catch a ride to Sumatra. They were a few days too late; the Japanese were waiting. With no strength to fight, the men were taken prisoner as Judy escaped back into the jungle.

For months, with the Brits now in captivity, Judy remained hidden, foraging for whatever food she could find. Yet she didn't forget her crew. Everyday, when guards were not looking, she would sneak in and out of the prison camp. Her visits were like getting a letter from home. She was the only positive note in a place where rations were meager, rats plentiful, and treatment brutal.

In the fall of 1942, when the military prisoners were loaded into trucks for a four-day ride to a prisoner-of-war camp called Gloegoer One, Judy followed on foot. At one point, when the caravan stopped, she even found a way to jump into one of the trucks. During these days the only thing to buoy the spirits of now-hopeless men was the Pointer's loyalty.

Gloegoer One had once been a Dutch military camp housing a hundred Dutch soldiers. Now it would be home to more than a thousand prisoners. The heat was oppressive, there was little health care, and the rations were a single bowl of rice a day. Under the command of Colonel Banno, the Japanese saw the Allied prisoners as slave labor and the men were put to work clearing the jungle. For seemingly no reason, they cut huge trees, hauled them away, and then cut more. As the months dragged by, Judy stayed with the imprisoned seamen. She was there when they worked and snuck into camp to sleep with them at night. The guards cursed and kicked her and even tried shooting her, but in the finest of British Naval traditions, Judy would not abandon her crew.

One seaman, named Cousens, had a skill the Japanese desperately needed. He had once been a cobbler, and the terrain was hard on boots. Thus, Cousens was pulled off the jungle detail and given the tools needed to ply his former trade. He also began hiding leather scraps and giving them to Judy. On many days this was all the dog had to eat, but even as she suffered and her ribs all but poked through her body, she still remained with her men.

When not cutting trees the seamen were digging graves. As the months passed, the Brits dropped like flies. There was no escape route and no end in sight. Most of the living came to believe they would die in the jungle and be forever forgotten. Then just about the time they were going to give up, they would spot their dog. Like them, she was little more than skin and bones, but she still kept going. When she growled at guards who cursed her, it came to represent resistance; when she came and went as she pleased, it represented freedom; and when she caught a snake or rat and shared it with the men, the act represented compassion. There were times she would even sneak into the Japanese food stores and steal a bag of rice to take back to her crew. Thus she was doing everything in her power not just to survive but to keep the men alive as well.

After months of working in the oppressive heat, the

seamen hatched a plan to steal food. They grabbed and hid several sacks of rice in a hut. One night they were enjoying the extra rations when two guards walked in. Employing the butts of their rifles, the Japanese began to beat the Allied prisoners. A second later Judy rushed through the door carrying a human skull. She darted between her comrades and their attackers, dropped her trophy, and began to growl. The guards had a deep-seated fear of the spirits of the dead and the skull caused them to panic. Forgetting about the stolen rations, they turned their guns on Judy. The dog, sensing her mission was complete, raced from the hut and back into the Sumatran jungle dodging bullets along the way. After that episode all the guards began to shy away from the dog.

When Cousens died in the summer of 1942, Judy lost the one man she depended upon most, yet she still wouldn't leave the camp. She stayed even as things grew worse. Judy observed men beaten to within an inch of their lives and others placed in cages for days at a time under the blistering sun. As the year dragged on, hundreds of men died from malaria, dysentery, skin ulcers, worm infestations, and beriberi. And then, a British airman, Frank Williams, was found hiding in the jungle and something almost miraculous happened in a world where there was no hope. Not surprisingly, Judy was the first to notice.

Williams had grown up in Portsmouth, England. Raised by a widowed mother, he was a smart, shy lad who read books more than he played games. To serve a country he loved, he enlisted in the Royal Air Force. Too tall to become a pilot, Frank was shipped to Singapore to man one of the newest tools of war: radar. Placed in a hopeless situation, he escaped China only to be shipwrecked and wash up in Sumatra. When captured he was all but starving.

In the prison camp, Williams noted the English Pointer that came and went as she pleased. With rations cut below what they had been just weeks before, the men no longer felt they could afford to share any food with Judy and the dog was obviously starving. While he had every right to feel sorry for himself, Williams's heart was deeply touched by the dog's plight. In spite of his own weakened state, he offered Judy a portion of his maggot-infested rice.

Because the fearless Judy showed great disdain for the Japanese, Williams reasoned this attitude would soon lead to her death. Thus, simply to save her life, he began to train her using whistles. Eager to please the man sharing his food with her, Judy eagerly responded. When she heard a certain whistle, she raced into the jungle and hid. When she heard another she came back to Williams's side. In this way the imprisoned airman was able to keep her out of harm's way.

Now that Williams had taught Judy the skills needed to avoid Japanese detection, she embraced this new skill to help Williams and the other prisoners. When the guards were in one area of the camp, she would go to another and steal their rations. She would then wait until she heard the "safe" whistle and bring a sack of stolen food to Williams who would share it with others. She also noticed men picking and eating fruit while on work details and began collecting fruit and sneaking it into camp. Yet because she was turning into such a lifesaver, Judy was also getting closer and closer to having the guards send out a hit squad to end her life.

Because there were tribes in the area who had pets, Judy likely ran into one of their dogs during her time searching for fruit. The result was a pregnancy. The starving prisoners, touched by her condition, shared even more food during this time in order to give the expectant mother a chance at delivering her babies. When the puppies arrived, Williams sensed an opportunity to give Judy a much better chance of survival.

Colonel Banno spent his off-duty hours visiting a woman who lived in a nearby village. When the commander's mistress came to camp, she always smiled each time she spotted Judy. Several times she even asked to pet the unique-looking dog. As soon as the pups were weaned, Williams picked one up and marched to Banno's office. Breaking every military protocol, he walked in unannounced and, while the colonel was on the phone, dropped the puppy in the middle of his desk. As the startled man hung up and rose from his chair, fists clenched, Williams explained the pup would be the perfect gift for the commander's mistress. As Banno's hands relaxed and his frown turned to a smile, the British airman then added a condition: he wanted Judy protected from the guards. Williams reasoned the best way to do this was make the dog an official prisoner of war. Banno looked at the puppy and then the bold prisoner, picked up a pen, and quickly filled out a form granting Judy of Sussex official prisoner-of-war status. She was now Prisoner of War 81A Gloegoer.

Now, as long as Banno remained in charge of the camp, Judy no longer had to fear the guards. She also had access to a daily food ration. But when Banno was transferred and Captain Nissi arrived, things changed. Nissi saw no need for a dog in camp. In fact, he viewed Judy as a potential meal for a banquet. When he caught her with Williams he went so far as to pull out his gun to shoot Judy. Before the shot could be fired, Williams produced the form Banno had filled out making Judy Prisoner of War 81A. Nissi, a stickler for military protocol, put his weapon away and allowed Judy to continue to have free reign of the camp. For months this arrangement kept the dog safe, but things dramatically changed in June 1944 when the Japanese were losing the war.

After spending almost the entire Pacific war in the Sumatran jungle, the prisoners were notified they were being transferred to Singapore. With a cruel smile on his face, Nissi pointed out that Judy was a prisoner of war only as long as she stayed in Gloegoer. Once she left camp she could be shot for attempting an escape.

Williams had a real problem. Without his presence, he was sure Judy would be killed. So he had to find a way to get her onto the prison ship. During his remaining nights in camp, the airman taught Judy to jump into a sack on command, and once she was in the bag to play dead. On transfer day, when the men went to the dock and were ordered to board the SS *Van Waerwijck*, Williams gave the signal. Judy raced to the sack and jumped in. Closely surrounded by fellow prisoners, the airmen smuggled the dog on board. The group was then led deep into the ship's hold as the *Van Waerwijck* put out to sea.

Not long after it departed on the afternoon of June 26 the *Van Waerwijck* was spotted by the HMS *Truculent*. Not realizing the ship was carrying hundreds of Allied prisoners, the submarine took aim and released a barrage of torpedoes. One scored a direct hit.

As the *Van Waerwijck* broke apart, Williams opened a porthole and pushed Judy out. She landed with scores of other prisoners in the ocean. When Williams managed to escape the doomed ship, Judy was nowhere in sight. At that time he was sure his dog was dead, but that was anything but the case. In fact, Judy had turned into a canine Esther Williams.

A large number of the prisoners couldn't swim. Somehow Judy sensed this. With no training in lifesaving, she hurried to a drowning man and, as he held onto her neck, swam to floating debris and steadied the prisoner until he could secure a hold. Rather than stay with the man she had just saved, she swam among pools of burning oil to find other hapless prisoners. She continued to navigate the open seas, pulling drowning men to safety, until all those in that area had been saved. Only then, now more dead than alive, did she wearily drag herself from the ocean onto a floating piece of wood.

With the Singapore trip aborted, the prisoners were pulled from the water, placed on a different vessel, and returned to Sumatra. Once back at the prison camp, Judy was reunited with Williams. The happiness of that reunion was short lived. The Japanese, now running low on resources, needed coal. While Sumatra had coal, it was too deep inland to transport out. In an act of desperation, the prisoners were marched into the sweltering jungle and ordered to build a railroad. Carving an iron road through mosquito-infested swamps and over forested mountains was a death sentence for many. Their days began at seven and didn't stop until after dark. If the work slowed, the prisoners were beaten and rations were reduced. As one mile became two and two became ten, Judy kept pace. Doing her part, she caught snakes and rats and shared them with the prisoners. Frank Williams and his friends later said they would have given up without Judy. She may have now been little more than a bag of bones, but in her eyes they saw the will to survive. In a sense, she stood for resistance. She was not going to allow the Japanese to win. And her spirit kept energizing men who wanted to give up and die.

By the summer of 1945, the war in Europe was over, but it was still going strong in the Pacific. During these long hot days the prisoners had no idea if the Allies were winning or losing. They also had no concept that within a few hundred miles American planes were destroying the Japanese fleet. All the POWs knew was they had to keep building the railroad or they would die. The line somehow was extended twenty miles into the jungle, and along the way the tracks were littered with scores of unmarked graves.

The workload eventually took its toll on Williams. Raging with a fever and weighing well under one hundred pounds, he was tossed onto a bed. A Japanese guard then cruelly suggested that Judy be cooked as Williams's last meal. The dog, somehow sensing the danger she was in, raced into the jungle. Not having Williams's whistle to tell her when it was safe to come home, she hid for several days.

Without Judy, Williams lost his will to live. He was even debating taking his own life on the day the dog found her way to the camp hospital and snuck inside to the man's bed. As he looked into the feeble, hungry canine's brown eyes, Williams vowed to live for a few more days if for no other reason than to share his rations with Judy. Less than a week later the stubborn airman walked out of the facility and readied himself to once more work in the jungle.

The Japanese guards now called those who hadn't been killed building the railroad "the living dead." The reason for this moniker was obvious. The prisoners had dropped half their body weight. Their bones pushed their skin in ways that clearly revealed every facet of their skeletal structure. The same was true for Judy. She looked more like a ghost than a living being. Yet even in this condition some of the men and the dog would not give up. Even when prisoners dropped dead beside them and they were forced to dig graves, some kept going. Even when rations were cut to a half a bowl of rice a day, some found ways to survive. As long as the rebellious dog resisted her captors, so would some of the remarkable Brits.

On August 15, without notice and under the cover of darkness, the Japanese disappeared and the prisoners woke up to find they were alone. Confused, they sat in the heat wondering what had happened. A dozen theories were tossed out, but none were taken seriously until a few hours later when Allied soldiers marched into the camp and announced the war was over. The men who had somehow survived four years in the jungle prison camp were too sick with malaria and beriberi to manage more than a soft cheer. In fact, as the need for resistance was now over, they could barely stand. The marines who freed them that day cried as they offered food and medicine.

Days later the American ship SS *Atenor* arrived to take the prisoners home to England. But as he and Judy approached the vessel, a jubilant Williams noted a sign forbidding animals of any kind from boarding. He figured Judy had been loyal to Britain for eight years, it was time the British returned that favor. Williams and his buddies quickly devised a plan. Williams walked onboard while his friends held the dog. When Williams was safely on deck, a few English seamen created a disturbance to take all eyes off the gangplank. At that point Williams called Judy and she raced to his side. The pair then quickly disappeared below deck. Only when they were well out to sea did the airman reveal the dog's presence. By then it was too late to change course. Essentially, an English Pointer that had never been in Britain was on her way home.

It took months walking the English countryside and

eating normal-sized meals before Williams and his adopted dog were once again healthy. By then the canine POW's story had become the stuff of legend. Every newspaper in the UK had given her the spotlight. She was even presented the highest honor an English animal could receive: the Dickin Medal. With Williams by Judy's side, the following proclamation was read, "For magnificent courage and endurance in Japanese prison camps, which helped maintain morale among her fellow prisoners and also for saving many lives through her intelligence and watchfulness."

A few months later, Williams accepted a job in Africa and took Judy with him for this new adventure. They remained side by side until her death in 1950. Williams erected a marble monument at her grave complete with a plaque that read, "A remarkable canine.... A gallant old girl who, with a wagging tail, gave more in companionship than she ever received...and was in her short lifetime an inspiration of courage, hope, and a will to live, to many who would have given up in their time of trial, had it not been for her example and fortitude." Judy was all that and more! In a moment in history where embracing resistance provided the only way to survive, she led the way.

Seven

Flight

The air up there in the clouds is very pure and fine, bracing and delicious. And why shouldn't it be?—it is the same the angels breathe.

—Mark Twain

Once you have filled your lungs with air, the will to live becomes a transforming force. Once you have been close to death, the empathy and concern you have for others is usually magnified. Once you have experienced loyalty, it is only natural that it be returned ten times over. In World War II, a German shepherd proved the validity of each of these secular proverbs. And while some dogs and a few humans might have equaled Antis's determination and fortitude, none have ever surpassed it.

On a bitterly cold night in January 1940, the war between the Axis powers and the Allies had come too close and a frantic family hurriedly grabbed what little they could carry and rushed through snow toward safety in France. In their hurry they forgot one of their prize dog's offspring. And now, as the hours alone grew into days, that puppy, hidden under a pile of discarded clothing, was nearing death.

A few miles away, Robert Bozdech held a camera in his hands as he and pilot Pierre Duval attempted to fly through ever-thickening morning fog. Driven out of his native land when the Nazis invaded in 1938, Bozdech was now fighting for France and tonight he had been assigned to do something he'd done on scores of other flights: to photograph German positions. Because he had survived so many high-risk missions, Bozdech was considered one of the luckiest men in the war, but on this night his luck would run out.

As their plane emerged from the fog, Duval noted a German fighter plane headed directly at them. Though the experienced French pilot attempted a quick turn, the Nazi war bird was far too fast for the aging Allied plane. In the blink of an eye, hot lead tore through the aircraft's thin metal skin sending Duval and Bozdech into a death spin. Somehow the pilot managed to hold the plane together until it hit the ground. The rough belly landing knocked out both men and the unguided aircraft plowed through a series of snowdrifts before coming to a halt in no-man's-land. The German infantry was a mile one way, the French a few miles in another direction, and the downed airmen were stuck in an area with no trees or cover.

Bozdech was the first to come to. After regaining his senses, he scrambled from the plane and searched the area for Nazi soldiers. When he found none, Bozdech pulled the still-groggy pilot from the wreckage. After the short, stocky Frenchman regained his senses, he begged his lean, lanky Czech friend to scramble to safety without him. The ever-loyal Bozdech stubbornly refused. Standing, he noted a farmhouse a few hundred yards away. After determining Duval was too badly injured to walk unaided, the gunner picked up his comrade and staggered through the snow toward the structure.

In the cold and wind, the short walk seemed like a marathon. A dizzy Bozdech was completely out of breath when he pushed the front door open and was greeted by a broken glass, a small table, a stove, and a few pieces of smashed furniture. Judging from the chaos before him, the gunner was quickly able to surmise that whoever recently lived here left in a hurry. Taking a deep breath, Bozdech counted his blessings that for the moment he and his pilot were safe. His plan was to just lay low for several hours, then when night fell again, if Duval had recovered enough to walk, they could make the risky crossing over open ground to French territory.

As Duval closed his eyes and rested, Bozdech checked out their hideaway. Though he figured the Germans could be just a few hundred feet away and hidden by trees, the area outside was clear. He snuck to the outbuildings to thankfully find them as void of life as the house. Grimly smiling, convinced that he and Duval's chances for avoiding capture had markedly improved, he pushed back through the snow toward the home. When he reentered the temporary haven, his sense of security was shattered. He heard a strange noise like a person crawling through the snow followed by barely perceptible breathing. His heart climbed up into his throat as he realized he had been wrong and they weren't alone!

Pulling his pistol from his belt, Bozdech demanded whoever was there to come out with their hands up. When there was no response he screamed out the orders again. The only reply was a series of light moans. Moving toward the sounds, the gunner kicked over a chair and pulled back a few pieces of discarded clothing to discover, wiggling on the floor, a shepherd puppy not more than four weeks old. It was emaciated and so weak it could barely move. He took a deep breath, nodded, and put his gun away. If he was going to share a home with a German, the Czech refugee was glad it was this one.

Bozdech had grown up around dogs and cats. When he was a child, his pets had taken the place of siblings. Thus, even in the midst of war, at a time when even his own fate was hanging in the balance, he felt great empathy for this pathetic creature. As he had done with small animals as a child, he whispered a few gentle words of reassurance before reaching down and scooping up the barely alive pup and bringing it up to his face. As the two stared at each other, Bozdech's heart melted. Pushing the half-dead puppy into his bomber jacket, he started a search for food. All he found were a few pieces of chocolate. After melting a little snow and softening the candy, he used his finger to force the liquid to the struggling German shepherd puppy's mouth. The famished animal eagerly licked the mixture from his hands. Over the next hour this action was repeated time and time again until the puppy fell asleep. Setting the animal on the floor, Bozdech relaxed and waited for nightfall.

Just after sundown, Bozdech shook Duval. It was time to see if the pair could crawl two miles across the snow to safety. As their lives depended on them making the perilous trek in complete silence, the puppy would have to be left behind. As he petted the German shepherd for a final time, Bozdech whispered a prayer that someone would find the tiny creature and adopt him even if that someone was a Nazi.

When the pair emerged from the house, the night was initially quiet. But within seconds of falling to their bellies and beginning their trek, the skies lit up with fire and the men found themselves in the middle of a battle. Digging even deeper into the snow, they crept forward. They made it only a hundred yards when the puppy awoke. Now alone and once again hungry, it began to cry. If any of the nearby German troops picked up on the sounds, the downed airmen would surely be spotted and become sitting ducks.

Duval was too badly injured to go back and silence the pup, so the responsibility fell upon Bozdech. Crawling through the snow, the gunner entered the house where he was greeted by an excited bundle of fur. This was not the time to play, so the man sadly shook his head and searched the room for something he could employ to mercifully end the pup's excited yelps. He decided that clubbing the German shepherd with a heavy object was the best choice. After finding a large rock just outside the door, he positioned the now-trusting dog on the floor and lifted his arm. Just as he was about to deliver a fatal blow, the tiny creature wagged its tail. Though Bozdech had grown to enjoy knocking Nazi planes from the sky, he didn't have the will or the strength to kill this German. Cursing his lack of courage, he picked the dog up and stuffed it into his jacket. He then slowly crawled back to his friend.

It took the men several excruciating hours to cover the two miles to the woods as they clawed through the snow on hands and knees. During this time the puppy didn't once cry out and give away their position. Only when they were in the safety of the French-controlled woods did the critter finally complain. As the injured Duval slept against a tree, Bozdech took his small charge from his jacket, held it in his glove-covered hands, and whispered, "We're safe!" He was still stroking the creature's tiny head when a French patrol found them a few minutes later.

Duval was hustled back to the road and quickly transported to a hospital to treat several broken bones. Bozdech and the puppy were examined and fed and then taken to an airfield where a single-engine plane was waiting. Bozdech, who had flown during his stint in the Czech Air Force, was ordered to get in the mechanized bird and hurry back to his base. As the small aircraft left the ground it would mark the first time the dog would fly, but it would not be the last. Once in the air, the still-unnamed pup rested in the pilot's lap, yawned, and went to sleep. He was so relaxed it was as if the sky was his natural environment.

Bozdech roomed with seven other refugee Czech airmen now flying for the French. Because he was long overdue from his mission, they were scared that their friend had died. So when Bozdech returned to the base the men threw an impromptu party that included warm milk for the pup. As they took turns holding the new arrival, they debated on a name. It was finally decided to christen the German shepherd after the plane they had first learned to fly in Czechoslovakia: the Pe-2. The small fighter had been nicknamed after a common insect. So the pup was now known as Ant.

Over the next few weeks the flyers spoiled the dog with food and love and Ant grew to appreciate each of the men. But there was no doubt which one drew his greatest affection and trust. Ant ate and slept with Bozdech. When the man was in the room the dog followed his every move and listened to his every word. Whenever Bozdech left for a mission the dog also shadowed him to the plane. The pup would then wait by the runway until his master returned from each mission.

By the time the dog was two months old, Bozdech had trained Ant to sit, stay, and heel on command and the obviously intelligent pup never disobeyed an order. But on a cloudy, winter afternoon, a suddenly disturbed Ant ignored the man's commands for the first time. For seemingly no reason the pup's face looked skyward, ears erect, as his eyes locked onto the horizon. A confused Bozdech turned in the direction but saw nothing. He tried to get Ant to refocus, but the dog continued to keep his eyes fixed on the sky. Finally, after several minutes, the airman heard the hum of planes and then there were almost unperceivable dots on the horizon. A second later panic set in as Bozdech realized German bombers with a fighter escort were headed their way.

The Dornier Do 17 was a twin-engine light bomber that had the power to inflict heavy damage. Due to their thin frames, they were often described as flying pencils. As these lethal machines grew near, Bozdech grabbed Ant and dove into a trench. It would be the pair's home for the next two hours as the Nazis bombed the base into oblivion. The damage was so great that it would take more than a week to get the facility back into operation.

Not surprisingly, from that day forward, the flyers reacted when the pup stopped playing and turned his gaze skyward. The British and French who joined the Czechs at the base also quickly grew to trust the dog's ability to hear German planes. The instant Ant turned his gaze to the sky, they raced into the control towers to warn the base that an enemy assault that had not yet appeared on radar was coming their way.

Over the next few weeks, Ant saved countless lives and tens of thousands of dollars' worth of equipment by warning of Nazi air attacks well before they happened. Just before Christmas, on a night when Ant celebrated his first birthday, the unit failed to understand the reason the dog wanted out of the flyers' quarters. They continued to ignore his scratching at the door until they too heard the German bombers. As the men and dog raced outside, bombs rained down from the skies and people and equipment were blown in every direction. As Ant barked, Bozdech, less than a hundred feet from where a bomb landed, was thrown sideways and knocked out. When he came to the Nazi planes were gone and his dog was nowhere in sight.

Dazed and confused, bleeding from wounds caused by flying debris, an anxious Bozdech frantically searched through wrecked buildings and equipment in an effort to find the dog that he had now loved for almost a year. Ant was nowhere. As one day became two the likely truth grew to monstrous proportions: Ant had to be dead. Unable to eat and barely sleeping, blaming himself for not paying attention to his dog's warning, the flyer turned gunner continued to dig through wreckage. Now convinced his dog had died, at the very least the man wanted a body to bury.

Almost fifty hours after the attack in an area Bozdech had searched several times, two French mechanics were walking down the main runway assessing damage. On a mound of dirt they noted a thin, bleeding dog. As they grew closer they recognized the barely breathing German shepherd lying on its side as the Czech airman's mascot. As the animal was rushed to the hospital, word was sent to find Bozdech. When man and dog were reunited at the infirmary Ant fought to rise but couldn't. Nevertheless his tail managed a weak wag signaling that now things were going to be all right. A relieved and tearful Bozdech stayed by Ant's side that night but the next morning went to where the dog had been found.

As he followed the blood trail, the man discovered that Ant had been so close to a bomb blast that he'd been covered by tons of concrete. Bozdech then discovered a small hole beside a large slab of concrete. He noted the desperate signs of claw marks on the cement and in the dirt. As he scooped up pieces of skin and fur it became obvious that Ant had been buried for two days in complete darkness. During that time the dog refused to give up, using all his energy to push aside huge rocks, lumber, and even concrete to reach the surface. As the man considered the ramifications of that monumental act, he realized his dog had accomplished what should not have been possible. In silent awe, Bozdech returned to the infirmary and hugged an animal that had proved again his passion for life. That will was made even more obvious when, within a few weeks, Ant was back on his feet, serving as the advanced warning system for bombers and waiting by the runway during missions for pilots to return.

The French were fighting a battle they could not win and in time the Germans pressed the existing government to seek peace. With the Nazis on the march, Bozdech and the Czechs were ordered to evacuate to England. This meant a dangerous trek across France before the flyers finally arrived in Gibraltar.

Though the French Air Force was now essentially out of business, the Czechs were given another option. The British needed aviators and wanted the experienced airmen in England. Bozdech and his friends were given priority passage on a ferry leaving Gibraltar. Yet there was a problem. Dogs were not allowed. With no way to smuggle his beloved Ant on board, Bozdech hatched a plan. He would stand on the deck of the ship and, when it set out to sea, he would simply call to his dog waiting on the shore. When the call was made the loyal shepherd easily swam the half mile of open water. Once onboard, Ant was hidden in the hold. This deception worked perfectly until the Nazis attacked. While the boat was sinking, Bozdech had to transfer to another vessel. The dog was spotted as the airmen snuck him aboard, but thankfully this ship's crew was accommodating and looked the other way. In Liverpool was another even tougher obstacle. While England would allow Ant to enter, the dog would have to be quarantined for six months to assure he was not carrying any illness. On top of that, Bozdech would have to pay for boarding the dog during that time. With no money, the Czech refugee faced a dilemma with no solution. If he couldn't come up with the money for care and boarding, Ant would be put down.

Refusing to give up on a dog that had saved their lives on several occasions, the Czech flyers put their heads together and hatched an escape plan. They would hide Ant with luggage that was about to be lifted via crane. They would then wait for the netted load to be lowered onto the dock and pretend to look for their trunks. When the customs officials turned their backs, they would grab Ant, encircle him, and hurry off. Against all odds the deception worked and Bozdech was able to once again be reunited with the now fully grown canine.

While the RAF did allow the Czech's canine mascot to stay on the base, the canine's insect-like name proved troublesome. The Brits continually confused it with *aunt*. Thus, Bozdech opted to rechristen the dog Antis. It would be while using that name that the German shepherd grew into a symbol of loyalty and courage that would inspire first an air unit and then a nation.

The Czech refugee was proud of his new uniform and enjoyed being in Liverpool but was eager to get back in the air to fight an enemy that had taken both his country and the lives of many of his friends. Yet for the first few months in England Bozdech remained grounded and assigned to desk duties. Working in the day allowed the refugee flyer to get to know the city in the evening. He and Antis spent hours exploring the port and meeting its people. In the midst of a horrific war it was a carefree time filled with good food and company. One night, when the grounded flyer was escorting his dog and a date around Liverpool, Antis grew strangely still. When the hair on the dog's back rose up and he turned toward Europe, Bozdech knew what was about to happen. Even though there were no air raid sirens, he hustled his date to safety just before the German bombers arrived. With only Antis's warning, destruction rained from the skies destroying the buildings all around where Bozdech hid.

After the bombing ended, Bozdech made sure his date had a safe ride home and then went to work in the rescue process. He followed behind as Antis sniffed out trapped victims and, perhaps remembering when he had been buried after a bombing, began to dig through the rubble to free them. Over the course of the next few hours the man and the German shepherd found and rescued six victims including a small child. A dog that was supposed to be in quarantine had saved six lives in his adopted country. Exhausted, his paws bleeding from frantically digging through concrete, dirt, and rock, Antis had to be carried to a local vet where his injured feet were treated. By any name, this dog was special.

When Bozdech was finally cleared for air duty he transferred to the 311 Squadron in Suffolk. As had been the case in France, Antis would march out to the runway, watch the plane carrying his master take off, and then, while neither eating nor drinking, would wait for Bozdech to come back home. When the man and his crew climbed out of their Wellington bomber, Antis would then march out to greet them and offer his paw to each man as if congratulating them on a job well done.

Though 1940 had given way to 1941, the Americans had yet to enter the war and bomber runs over Germany were so dangerous that few who went on these missions lived to make more than a dozen raids. As Bozdech's mission count climbed and his skills as a gunner were revealed, he was transferred to East Wretham in Norfolk. There he was assigned to a Wellington Bomber code-named *C for Cecilia*. In June, on one of the first missions, as Antis stood on the runway and watched his master fly toward Germany, the dog seemed strangely despondent. In the early morning hours Antis, who had always remained mute during his waits, began to howl and cry. No one could calm him down. Hours later, as dawn broke and the planes came back to base, Antis's demeanor did not improve. The *Cecilia* was not on the horizon.

Initial reports coming in from the other flyers indicated that *C for Cecilia* had gone down on the run. The time the plane had been hit matched the moment Antis had begun to howl. So how had the dog known and how could they get the large German shepherd to give up his runway watch?

While generally accurate, as it was true *C for Cecilia* had been hit and badly damaged, the eyewitness accounts were wrong in one very important matter. The plane had not crashed but was slowly limping toward home. As the pilot struggled to keep the bomber airborne, Bozdech was leaning over his guns, blood dripping from a deep head wound. Growing weaker by the moment, thoughts of his dog kept him focused.

Somehow, through more will than mechanics, *C for Cecilia* limped across the English Channel and made it back to England. After withstanding a crash landing, Bozdech was rushed to a hospital where surgeons dug into his skull and saved his life. Twelve hours later, as news filtered back to the base that the crew was all right and the plane would be trucked back for repairs, a collective sigh of relief could be heard. But while the airmen and crews of the 311 celebrated, there was no way to explain to Antis that his master would in time be coming home. Heartbroken, the animal refused to eat or leave his place beside the runway. As a cold rain fell, a soaking-wet Antis stood and looked toward the sky.

Because it would be days before Bozdech would be released from the hospital, the 311 Squadron naturally was deeply worried about its mascot. Though the war was still raging and nightly raids were still being made, the flying band of brothers convinced the base chaplain to drive to the hospital where Bozdech was being treated. A few hours later, the uniformed clergyman returned with the injured flyer. It took Antis a few moments to understand that the heavily bandaged man limping toward him was indeed his master, but when recognition hit, the dog went crazy. After a wild dance of joy, Antis finally accepted a meal from Bozdech's hands. It was the first time he'd eaten for days. Though it was easy to see the dog was now satisfied that things were all right, no one could have guessed the German shepherd had already devised a plan to make sure he and Bozdech would never again be separated.

By the end of June, Bozdech was well enough to fly. This time he and the crew of his Wellington would be joined by more than a thousand other RAF planes on a midnight raid over northwest Germany. As he marched from the hangar, the gunner looked for his dog. Antis was nowhere to be found. Worried, Bozdech asked the ground crew to search for the German shepherd. Word spread and the base was turned upside down but Antis was AWOL. As *C for Cecilia* lifted off, Bozdech was a mental wreck. He was convinced his beloved pet had somehow been killed.

An hour later, as the Wellington flew over Europe, Bozdech took his position and checked his guns. As he undertook what had become a routine mental checklist, someone nudged his arm. He looked down at his feet and spotted his German shepherd. Somehow, at a heavily secured airbase, Antis had climbed into the plane and hidden in the gun turret where her master worked. Initially shocked to the point of experiencing a brain freeze, Bozdech suddenly realized they were flying at sixteen thousand feet and the heavily panting Antis needed oxygen. Unstrapping his own mask, the gunner pushed it over the dog's nose. They would share the oxygen for the rest of the mission.

That night *C for Cecilia* successfully deposited its bombs onto an oil refinery literally blowing the facility apart. As the Wellington Bomber turned to head home the plane was met with antiaircraft flack from the ground and Nazi fighters in the air. Everything that was fired at the bomber miraculously missed. When *C for Cecilia* returned to East Wretham in perfect condition, Bozdech readied himself for a dressing down. He reasoned no one was going to believe he had nothing to do with Antis accompanying him on the mission. As the gunner waited to be lectured, his British commander studied the *Cecilia* and then eyed the dog before turning his back and walking off. When a confused Bozdech caught up and tried to explain what had happened, the officer mumbled something about not seeing a dog but the next time *C for Cecilia* took off that dog he didn't see better be equipped with its own oxygen mask.

Over the next year Antis became both a hero and

a British national treasure. The dog was featured in newspaper stories and in newsreels. With each new mission to Germany, he inspired a beleaguered English nation to continue to fight. But though he was glorified in the media, Antis was anything but an active participant in the raids. He simply climbed on board, had his oxygen mask placed on him, settled in under Bozdech's feet, and went to sleep. Even as bullets ripped through the Wellington's skin, he never moved. When the night lit up with fire and the concussion from exploding bombs rocked the airplane, Antis continued to snooze. Bozdech and the crew would often point to the dog's calm assuredness as a factor in their success. It was hard to panic when Antis was so confident in the men's ability to accomplish their mission and bring the ship home.

At the conclusion of a particularly hard battle with German fighters, on a night when *C for Cecilia*'s fuselage absorbed thousands of rounds, the true cost of war was revealed. Though he'd never as much as whimpered during the long raid, Antis had been struck several times by shrapnel. A bit of minor surgery was all that was needed and the dog was back in the plane for the next mission. Three flights later the dog was hit again, and this time the injuries were much more serious. The head wound left one of his ears bent, thus giving the dog the look of an unsuccessful pugilist. Though they always sent men with this type of injury back into the air, those in charge of the 311 Squadron decided to ground the dog. He was simply too valuable a symbol to the squad and the British people to be lost.

Bozdech now had a real problem. Antis panicked whenever *C for Cecilia* took off without him. Thus, the flyer was going to have to provide the canine with a new mission. After discovering a four-year-old girl named Jennifer, whose father had been killed during the early days of the war, Bozdech introduced his dog to the child. The sad little girl and the injured dog immediately bonded. From that point forward Bozdech took Antis to Jennifer before he left on a mission. It was an arrangement that helped a grieving child and took away a dog's worries.

When the US finally entered the war, Bozdech and his crew were given a US-made Liberator bomber. With four huge engines and incredible firepower, they were assigned to seek out Nazi U-boats and sink them. Due to his new mission, the Czech refugee spent the remainder of World War II cruising over the North Sea and the Atlantic Ocean looking for what flyers called fish.

As was his nature, Antis, even when he was with Jennifer, found ways to amuse himself. The German shepherd snuck out to chase sheep, pulled wet garments from clotheslines, and even riled up a local constable. Yet each time he got into trouble, his amazing military record and his unique skill of sensing air raids came back to save him.

It wasn't until the war ended that Antis finally got the chance to fly again. This time he climbed into a Liberator bomber with Bozdech on a flight to Czechoslovakia. Not surprisingly, the Czechs who flew for the RAF and their mascot were greeted as heroes.

Experiencing peace for the first time in years, Bozdech settled back into civilian life. The young man fell in love, married, and became a father. For almost three years he lived a charmed life with Antis always by his side. Then, when the USSR took over his homeland in 1948, the invaders began to arrest and imprison all Czechs who had been a part of the British Armed Forces during World War II. Just like a decade before, Bozdech was forced to gather a few comrades, pack what he could carry on his back, and, this time with Antis leading the way, leave his home and family under the cover of darkness. On foot the small band made its way toward West Germany. At least a half dozen times they would have been discovered and arrested if the dog had not alerted them to nearby Russian forces. Simply by trusting Antis's special radar they managed to escape, but sadly that meant that Bozdech and his dog were once again refugees.

The Czech and his German shepherd immigrated to England. Sadly, due to the nature of the Cold War and his desire to protect them from possible imprisonment, Bozdech never again saw his family. A year after they settled into their new home, Antis was awarded the nation's highest canine honor: the Dickin Medal. With proper British ceremony, a military officer cited Antis for exceptional bravery, loyalty, and sacrifice. As a newspaper reporter who covered the event noted, Antis was a dog that could fly.

In 1953, more than thirteen years after he was rescued from a crumbling house between German and French lines, Antis died. Though he would live another thirty-three years, Robert Bozdech would never again own a dog, proving that loyalty works both ways, and each time he looked to the sky he would think of the dog that loved to fly.

Eight

Bond

The bond that links your true family is not one of blood, but of respect and joy in each other's life.

—Richard Bach

In the history of literature no sailor is likely as famous as Sinbad. This fictional Middle Eastern oceanic adventurer has been thrilling audiences for six centuries. In absorbing and fanciful tales he took on monsters of the deep and superhuman villains from the land. He was a source of inspiration for those who had no hope and one of the greatest reservoirs of joy for readers who longed for excitement. He became such a legend that movies presented his exploits and even a cartoon character sang a song about Sinbad the Sailor. Yet when these tales were created and first published, it is highly unlikely that anyone foresaw a dog that for a while would become as famous as his Arabian namesake.

In the cold winter of 1937, the US Coast Guard Cutter *Campbell* was docked in New York City. Chief Boatswain's Mate "Blackie" Rother was visiting a close friend when he happened upon a small brown, black, and white dog of dubious lineage. After discovering the mutt had no home, he cleaned the canine up and headed to his girlfriend's apartment. What the well-meaning but ignorant Rother didn't know would quickly come back to bite him as well as change the course of Coast Guard history. It seemed the apartment house the woman called home did not allow pets. So rather than greet the barking, wiggling bundle of fur with enthusiasm, the girlfriend frowned and ordered the gift returned to the crowded, hostile city streets. Most men of that time would have likely dropped the mutt in the nearest alley, and, after perhaps giving the creature a friendly pat on the head, waltzed off into the night. But Rother was not most men. In just two hours he had grown to genuinely love the critter. He was not going to leave the Big Apple without securing a home for the canine waif. Yet with his leave running out he had little time to make his pitch and those friends he did track down refused to adopt the twenty pounds of happiness.

The *Campbell* was leaving in hours for duty at sea and, having no place to put the unwanted gift, Rother hid the dog in his duffle bag, snuck past those on watch, and quickly made his way to the ship's main berth deck. There he pulled the critter out and showed the homeless mutt to the other sailors. The dog possessed a personality three times the size of his body. In the span of ten minutes, with his bright eyes, wagging tail, intelligence, and seemingly thoughtful expression, he'd charmed all of those present. Ah, but a ship was not a democracy. Just because the sailors sleeping in the main berth deck wanted to keep the dog, there was still the question of whether the captain would allow him to stay onboard. Rather than risk an order to take the dog back to shore, the men convinced Rother to keep the mongrel hidden until the *Campbell* was well out to sea. With that plan in place the crew smuggled some food from the mess, and as the dog ate the men discussed names. A dozen were tossed out, but it was Sinbad that stuck.

The first night went well. Sinbad made no noise and slept like a baby. Yet at just past six bells, as the men were assembling on the deck for muster, the dog began to bark. The Chief Boatswain's Mate had a bit more pull than other seamen, so when Sinbad announced his presence Rother explained the situation. After laying out the facts, he then implied that, because of circumstances, the dog was meant to be on the *Campbell*. It was as if ordained by Providence. Unimpressed, the captain demanded Sinbad be brought up on deck. As the dog sat at the officer's feet, the man in charge made a full inspection complete with several deep belly scratches. With the anxious crew looking on, he then stood and announced Sinbad could stay if the dog learned the discipline needed for a life at sea. If that were not accomplished during the week, he would be put off at the first port of call.

Over the course of the next seven days the sailors took turns hurrying their new mascot through obedience training. He was taught to stay, sit, shake, and speak. Sinbad also learned to recognize when men were on duty and off, as well as being taught what parts of the ship would always be off limits to the pooch. Showing intelligence the men did not expect, the dog quickly mastered the skills needed to be a part of the crew. At the next port of call Sinbad was even allowed to leave with Rother and his friends to visit some local eating establishments, but more important, was also welcomed back on when the leave was over.

As the ship's mascot, Sinbad developed some unique habits that fully cemented his standing as a seaman. He preferred the company of regular sailors to officers. In fact, when carried into the captain's room for visits, he darted out as quickly as his feet hit the floor. He loved navy chow, drank black coffee each morning with his breakfast, and was known to share a drink or two with his comrades when on shore leave. In fact, he became a regular visitor to the bars and saloons at various ports of call. He also had his own hammock. He even learned to drag his bag out for inspections. The dog assembled each morning with the men, stood for roll call, and in time was assigned a duty station.

During his first year on the *Campbell*, it was decided that Sinbad was such an important part of the crew he needed to become an official member of the US Coast Guard. The crew filled out enlistment papers signed with a paw print and sent them in to Washington. Seeing this as good publicity, the Coast Guard returned the enlistment document with a request for a service record and a photo. When everything was completed Sinbad was issued a service number and a card that allowed him to visit the Red Cross stations around the globe. His rank was Sea Dog 1st Class.

Due to his official status and the Coast Guard's publicity machine, the little pooch was soon featured in both newsreels and magazine stories. Wherever and whenever the *Campbell* docked, newspaper reporters turned out to snap Sinbad's picture as well as gain an interview, which in most cases meant a bark from the canine and a few words of praise from a crewman. As his fame grew, Sinbad was given the key to cities, met mayors, and was toasted at bars on both sides of the Atlantic. His favorite port was Londonderry, Ireland, where locals were always ready with biscuits and the Red Cross Station treated him like royalty. It was also Londonderry where Sinbad was given an appreciation banquet at the historic Guild Hall. There, dressed in their finery, men and women who were already fighting World War II united to forget battles and revel in the antics of a sea dog.

What was displayed at the banquet in Ireland in essence defined Sinbad's life. He was not heroic in the nature of other war dogs; he was, rather, a member of a crew. Like a misguided teen, he didn't spin around on command, never saluted officers, and was not any good at taking written messages from one part of the 320-foot-long ship to the other. During rough weather, he didn't battle the waves that spilled over the deck or athletically balance on the bridge as the vessel rolled; he went below to his bunk. His jobs were simply to offer relief from long hours of boredom, to provide a sense of family to those who were homesick, and generate a few laughs when worn spirits had all but given out. The one thing of real canine value Sinbad was known for was playing with a large metal washer. The crew would roll the washer along the deck and the dog would retrieve it. After that game lost its allure, a seaman would place the washer on Sinbad's nose and he would toss it up into the air and catch it in his mouth. It was the latter trick that fascinated bar patrons on both sides of the Atlantic and led to the men of the *Campbell* being treated to rounds of free drinks.

The first blemish on Sinbad's record occurred in frigid waters. Just after Denmark had fallen to Nazi Germany in World War II, the *Campbell* was ordered to sail to Greenland. The Coast Guard cutter's mission was to make sure the Germans did not set up any type of bases on this Danish-owned piece of land. Fearing occupation by the Nazis, those who lived in this little known and frigid world welcomed the visitors with open arms. Though there was little to see, the Americans did their best to enjoy a region with far more snow and ice than people while counting their blessings that the US was not having to wage war.

As always, Sinbad was sent ashore with the first landing party. After frequenting a few pubs with his mates, he decided to explore. Because he had been born in one of the world's largest cities and raised on a ship, the dog was likely not prepared for the rural environment that now beckoned him. In the summer, Greenland's wide-open spaces were filled with grazing sheep. With few predators, most of these sheep wandered from hillside to valley without supervision. Likely not understanding what these creatures were, Sinbad raced up to meet them causing the flock to run away. This game continued throughout the afternoon with the only breaks coming when the dog returned to town to get something to eat and grab a bit of sleep. Once he was completely refreshed and sporting a full belly, Sinbad then returned to the country and his version of the game of tag.

Over the course of a week, the most famous dog in the US Coast Guard chased hundreds of sheep and in time the game Sinbad was playing became deadly. The dog literally ran a half dozen sheep so hard they died. Hundreds of others grew so nervous they quit eating. When caught in the act, angry farmers returned the dog to town, and sailors spirited him out of the jail and smuggled him back to the *Campbell*. This action literally saved the dog's life. If he'd been detained on shore the farmers of Greenland would have demanded he be put to death. This episode marked one of the first times in US history that Uncle Sam also paid the bill for the death of sheep during "combat."

Over the next four months, with only a rotating skeleton crew keeping watch on the *Campbell*, the men of the ship grew close to the people of Greenland. They learned to enjoy the food, the area's unique games, and the harsh weather. But as World War II engulfed all of Europe, the cutter was needed as a symbol of American power in other areas. As a gesture of defiance to the Axis powers, in October 1940, the

Campbell set sail for Lisbon, Portugal. The large, white ship would spend almost a half year in the old European port as a reminder to Hitler that one wrong move could bring another major player into the war.

During his stay in the place Christopher Columbus had once lived, Sinbad was again granted shore leave. Over the course of the winter and into the early spring, the dog went along with crewmates on tours of villages, wineries, farms, museums, and castles. He walked along roads that were built by the Romans and entertained hundreds with his washer trick. Yet after an extended tour of Portugal, when a group of American sailors returned to the port of Lisbon, the dog began to mournfully bark. A few seconds later the sailors understood why Sinbad was so upset; the *Campbell* was no longer in port. As the panicked men raced down the dock, a local sailor caught them and explained a hurricane was headed their way and the cutter had sailed out to sea in an attempt to avoid the storm's wrath. Meanwhile the city was battening down the hatches and folks along the shore were headed for higher ground. He suggested the Americans run the other way and look for shelter.

As the seamen headed on foot back toward Lisbon, Sinbad, his eyes fixed on where he knew the *Campbell* was supposed to be, didn't move. With his feet planted firmly on the dock's wooden planks, again and again he refused to follow when called. Sensing the dog was not going to obey orders, the men picked up a crying Sinbad and carried him back to the city where they discovered businesses closed, doors locked, and the streets deserted. As the winds grew stronger and the rains began, the sailors finally found refuge in a hotel. For hours, with Sinbad hiding under a bed, the hurricane rocked the coast and shook the building to its foundation. While windows broke, doors flew open, and water filled the streets, those in the hotel survived. Once the skies cleared, Sinbad and the men made the long trek back to the docks. The wreckage they observed was horrifying. Some ships had been pushed hundreds of feet up onto the shore and others were resting on the sides in the bay. Silently, worried that the *Campbell* might have suffered the same fate, the sailors looked toward the sea. As the hours passed the Americans' spirits dropped. Then as the sun set Sinbad grew excited. He paced back and forth and barked. Suddenly hopeful, the men looked toward the horizon but saw nothing. Finally, while peering through binoculars one of the sailors was able to spot their cutter steaming toward Lisbon. After he shared the news, he looked down at Sinbad. How had the dog known the *Campbell* was safe and headed back to its assigned port? He couldn't have seen it, so had he heard the ship or had he sensed it? Though often debated by the crew, no one would ever know how the dog had realized the ship was on its way home.

From Lisbon the *Campbell* headed to Sicily and as usual Sinbad was the first to hit the shore when the ship docked, but when it came time to leave the dog wasn't there. With orders to embark, the cutter headed back to the United States without the mascot. Several hours later men assigned to a navy destroyer discovered Sinbad on the dock. The

US Navy brought the dog back to the States where he was reunited with his concerned crew.

Another time, when leaving a US port, Sinbad again didn't make it back to the *Campbell* before the ship left. He was spotted while the vessel was still in the harbor and a launch was sent to pick him up. On that occasion the captain declared the canine AWOL and tossed him in the brig for a couple of days.

When the *Campbell* was assigned to sail to Casablanca, the dog once again hit the shore with the first landing party. When the men assigned to watch him ducked into a bar, Sinbad explored the city until finally getting picked up by the city's dogcatcher. The *Campbell* was about to depart when the crew heard barking and noted the dog was racing toward the ship being chased by a man with a net. When the city official and the captain met, they shared their stories. It seemed that Sinbad's chasing cats and begging for food had led to his arrest. Then when the dog heard the ship's whistle blow he found a way to escape. After being assured the canine sailor would never again be let loose in Casablanca, the dogcatcher allowed the captain to take Sinbad on board.

On another occasion the dog was roaming in Ireland and, as was now becoming routine, didn't make it back in time for departure. The *Campbell* was over a half mile away from the dock when the dog appeared. As Sinbad furiously barked, the crew looked toward the captain. This time he shook his head and forbade a launch being used to pick up the animal. Realizing he was not going to be retrieved,

Sinbad jumped into the water and began to swim. As he watched the animal frantically move through the water, the captain cursed, shook his head, and signaled for two of the sailors to go back and get the mascot in a launch. The long swim before he was plucked from the water must have made an impact; this would be the last time Sinbad was late for departure.

While the missions across the Atlantic were always eventful, after December 7, 1941, they grew to be tense. In the course of just one day the mood changed, as did the routine. The *Campbell* was even repainted from white to gray and transferred to the US Navy. It was now a noisy den of activity that never shut down. And whenever anyone was on the deck, all eyes were on the water. Gun drills were conducted daily, discipline became more rigid, and shore leave was rare.

As the US plunged more deeply into war, Sinbad's role became more important. It was the dog that offered a break from the concerns and the worries of battle. Each time they saw the black, tan, and white mascot, it was almost like getting a letter from home. During the war men actually lined up to spend time with Sinbad and they sometimes drew lots to see who would get to feed him or have him sleep with them in their bunks. His antics provided a valuable source of entertainment and just the act of petting him brought a sense of security.

As the war dragged on, the *Campbell* was assigned for convoy escort duty. When cargo and troop ships made their long, slow Atlantic crossing, the Coast Guard cutter was the guard dog. It would sniff out German U-boats and take them on as the convoy moved away to safety. During these battle operations, Sinbad had a custom-made helmet strapped onto his small head and was taken below. There he waited for the hostilities to end so he could return to deck and survey the damage.

As skirmishes and battles came more often, the crew began to see Sinbad as a good luck charm. While other escort ships had been heavily damaged or sunk, the *Campbell* was a floating version of Superman; it fought, won, and then steamed away with only minor bruises. On February 22, 1943, as the ship battled the seas in the North Atlantic, that all changed. Through a light drizzle and fog, a German sub somehow snuck into position unnoticed. Before being spotted, the U-boat managed to launch a single torpedo that hit a Norwegian steamer. The ship was headed to the bottom as its crew jumped out into the frigid waters. The *Campbell* moved into position to rescue survivors only to discover the attack had been a ruse. The U-boat had hit the freighter as a way of getting the cruiser to slow down and move into range. With the sub on the surface, its crew opened fire and the *Campbell* responded in kind. Turning directly toward the Nazi U-boat, the cutter forced the sub to dive. After dropping depth charges and noting a large oil slick, the *Campbell* returned to its position guarding the convoy.

Ever wary and now very much on guard, the *Campbell* didn't just stake out a position and hold it. Instead it circled the convoy using every possible means to study the waters for the enemy. As the men focused on their instruments and used field glasses, Sinbad took a position next to one of the main guns. On this night the jovial dog was as quiet and focused as the crew. With his helmet still in place, the dog seemed ready for action.

It was just after seven when the cutter spied another U-boat periscope. Changing course, the *Campbell* sped directly at the sea wolf. As the sub dropped into the deep, depth charges were released. One directly hit the German vessel. It appeared the battle had been won, but while the men celebrated, their dog remained tense. When one of the men spotted a second sub, the crew understood what Sinbad had somehow heard or sensed. On this night the German U-boats were operating in a pack.

The next hour saw the *Campbell*'s guns blazing as the crew fought a war on the ocean's surface followed by dropping scores of depth charges. Based on oil slicks the cutter destroyed at least four U-boats in the course of the battle. Yet Sinbad, who was still on the deck, was not in a celebratory mood. His senses proved once more correct as another German sub surfaced and opened fire.

The *Campbell* rapidly changed course and headed right toward the enemy vessel. The U-boat was just edging below the surface when the cutter's crew dropped the depth charges. As huge plumes of water rose skyward, the sub was hit. The damaged U-boat fought toward the surface in an attempt to limp away, but the Nazi captain took the wrong course. As the *Campbell's* crew looked for their opponent, the ship surfaced directly in front of the cutter. They were too close to avoid a collision so the captain called out for more speed and a few seconds later the *Campbell* cut the U-boat in half. As the crew celebrated, Sinbad moved from his spot beside the gun to the port side of the ship. He looked worried and the crew would soon find out why. There was a huge gash in the *Campbell's* hull and unless it was quickly patched, the ship would go down.

Several members of the crew dove into the frigid water to assess and address the damage. Yet even as they worked, the engine room flooded and the cutter went dark. Dead in the water, it was now an easy target for any type of enemy vessel. Men held their breath as the work crew fought cold and odds in an attempt to seal the hole. Within an hour they had done so, but by this time the convoy and other escort ships were well out of sight. As they still couldn't get the engines operational, they were sitting ducks.

As Sinbad paced from one end of the ship to the other, the *Campbell* radio operator called for help. A British tug heard the distress call and steamed toward the badly injured American cutter. At the same time, the *Burza*, a Polish destroyer, received the call and also changed course to meet the ship. As the Coast Guard crew waited for the much needed help, they looked out at the water wondering if there was still one more U-boat under the surface targeting them.

For a dog that had little regard for officers, Sinbad did a strange thing on this night; he followed along on the heels of the *Campbell's* commander. Perhaps the dog's new loyalty was out of concern, since the man in charge of the cutter was sporting several obvious shrapnel wounds, but more likely it was Sinbad understanding that the crew's fate depended upon this person's leadership. It was while looking at the dog that the captain finally and assertively yelled to his men, "Relax, as long as Sinbad is on the *Campbell* she will not sink." While this might not have been as memorable as John Paul Jones declaring, "We have not yet begun to fight," it nevertheless worked its magic. The crew immediately gained an air of confidence.

When the *Burza* arrived, the majority of the *Campbell's* crew was transferred to the Polish ship, but Sinbad remained on the damaged cutter. When a sailor attempted to take the dog to the destroyer, the captain waved him off explaining that the dog had to be on the cutter to assure that it would not sink. Only when the tug arrived and latched on to the *Campbell* did Sinbad finally head below deck to his bunk.

When the *Campbell* made it back to the United States there was a huge contingent of press waiting on the dock. When the captain was asked how the ship managed to do so much damage to the German wolf pack and survive ramming what had now been identified as *U-606*, the ship's leader pointed to Sinbad and explained, "The dog inspired us and pulled us through." In a feature story, *Life* magazine summed up the furry hero in these words, "A liberty-rum-chow-hound, with a bit of bulldog, Doberman pinscher, and what-not."

Already well known before this battle, Sinbad now emerged as such a huge celebrity that while the *Campbell* was being repaired, the dog went on a nationwide recruiting tour. It was estimated that thousands joined the military thanks to meeting the once-unwanted mutt. Sensing a public relations gold mine, the Coast Guard quickly tossed together a book describing his exploits, *Sinbad of the Coast Guard*.

Sinbad, even with his star status, was on the deck of the *Campbell* when it put back out to sea. By the time the cutter arrived in New Orleans for shore leave, the mascot had been elevated from Dog 1st Class to Chief Dog. It would be a short-lived promotion. At a public ceremony to honor his new rank, Sinbad broke away, ran through the legs of several members of the press, raced down the dock, and disappeared into the city. When he finally returned several days later, he was booked for having been AWOL, had his rank reduced, and was confined to the brig until the cutter was again at sea.

Yet even though he was back to just being a Dog 1st Class, Sinbad remained a part of the *Campbell*'s crew until the end of the war. And with the dog on board, in battles in both the Atlantic and the Pacific, the ship's luck held firm as it was never damaged so badly it was sunk. Those who sailed on the *Campbell* swore it was the dog that kept the ship afloat.

Two years later, while the canine was still on active duty, Hollywood made a film about Sinbad's war exploits. The tie to the original stories of Sinbad the Sailor tales was obvious in the title Universal Pictures chose. *Dog of the Seven Seas*, while not a hit, was one of the most unusual releases of the year and served as a platform to keep Sinbad's name in the press.

Two years later, in 1949, the ship's captain decided the dog was too old for life at sea and Sinbad was sent to the Coast Guard's Barnegat Light Small Boat Station. He would remain there until his death on December 30, 1951. The next day, on New Year's Eve, Sinbad was buried with full military honors at the base of the station's flagpole. The obituary that ran in newspapers around the globe noted that while Sinbad had never again risen beyond Dog 1st Class, he had earned the American Defense Service Medal, American Campaign Medal, the European-African-Middle Eastern Campaign Medal, the Asiatic-Pacific Campaign Medal, the World War II Victory Medal, and the Navy Occupation Service Medal. Few sailors could claim all those ribbons.

In the end, Sinbad was not a war dog that ever saved a life and didn't actually provide any vital function to the ship on which he served. All he did was offer friendship, loyalty, and a sense of security. It was the latter that might have led to the *Campbell* becoming one of the US Coast Guard's most valuable ships. From sinking subs to successfully guiding nineteen convoys across the Atlantic, there was one constant. While the human crews rotated, a once-unwanted dog remained in place as an unsinkable symbol of the bond of the men who served on the sea.

NINE

VALUE

You must look within for value, but must look beyond for perspective.

—Denis Waitley

If not for the successful television series *M*A*S*H*, the Korean War might well be almost forgotten today along with the more than thirty-three thousand who died in what was officially called a "conflict" or "police action." Often referred to as the forgotten war, more than six decades later few know how it started or why and yet the deep wounds between north and south still fester. What happened in Korea changed the world in a dramatic way as it revealed then and continues to expose the fragility of peace in the nuclear age.

In the final weeks of World War II, just two days after President Harry Truman ordered the atomic bomb dropped on Hiroshima, the USSR finally declared war on a now-completely crippled Japan. The reason for Stalin's declaration was not to enter into the fighting but rather to claim some of the spoils. And what happened with Russia's entry into war on August 8, 1945, continues to resonate. Due to Soviet influence, Korea, which had been under Japanese rule for decades, was split into two separate nations with neither the north or the south recognizing the legitimacy of the other. With the American eagle anchored in the south and the Russian bear in the north, the cold war was birthed even as the celebration of the conclusion of World War II continued.

In an effort to keep a watchful eye on Russian influence, the United States, which already had a large military presence in occupied Japan, stationed troops in South Korea. For several years those who drew this assignment were little more than policemen. They kept their comrades in line and attempted to prevent theft of supplies from American bases. They were not very successful. In a nation racked with poverty and hunger, goods continued to disappear from warehouses at an alarming rate. A frustrated US decided that if humans were unable to stop the theft then they would put that task in the paws of man's best friend. On orders from the Pentagon a hundred dogs were called into active sentry duty. With the canines acting as living burglar alarms crime was all but eliminated.

As thousands of homesick men fought loneliness and boredom, the sentry dogs also soon served as morale officers and friends. As the bond between GI and dog grew, another alliance was being forged that would lead to the sentry canines being completely wiped out and war once more threatening to erupt across the globe.

An alliance between communist Chinese forces and North Korea helped turn the tide in the Chinese civil war. In late 1949, when the forces of Mao Zedong drove the armies of Chiang Kai-shek from the mainland and established communist rule in China, it shook both Washington and London. Stalin and his confederates now controlled almost half the globe and were still looking to expand. The first real test of Western resolve came in Korea.

Emboldened by Mao's success, North Korean leader Kim Il-Sung planted and supplied more than ten thousand guerrilla fighters in South Korea. Though half were either killed or captured within a year, this underground army sowed seeds of fear among the South Korean population as it exposed the weakness of the fledgling democracy. As citizens voiced complaints about the US-backed government, Kim became convinced he had broad support in the south and leaned on the USSR and China for weapons. Those requests were granted and, behind a curtain of secrecy, North Korea prepared for a full-scale invasion.

The Chinese, who feared the large American presence in Japan, fully supported Kim's plans. By pushing the United States out of Korea, Chairman Mao could then turn his attention to expanding Chinese influence into Southeast Asia. Also, most Asian military minds believed that a North Korean invasion would reveal that the Americans had little stomach for another large war.

On June 25, 1950, in an attack for which the US and its allies were not prepared or expecting, seventy-five thousand

North Koreans pushed into the south. It was the sentry dogs that alerted the American military when the communist soldiers were in Seoul, but the alarm was sounded too late. With only small numbers of Americans on the ground and with a poorly prepared and disorganized South Korean military, unsure of what to do, there was no time to mount a resistance. Leaving the dogs behind, the US hurriedly retreated further south. While this move saved human lives, it left the trained canines in harm's way. Within hours almost all the American dogs had been apprehended and executed. Those that were not captured starved to death. Though thousands of Americans remained in South Korea trying to hold the remaining ground and repel the unexpected attack, there were no military dogs left to fight with them, and this would open the door to thousands of deaths that could have been prevented. Worse yet, in 1950, as the military moved toward the technological age, there were no field dogs ready for action.

Within days of North Korea's initial attack, the United Nations met and agreed to support the troubled South Korean defenses. By August the first combat-ready American troops deployed from Japan and entered the war. Under the command of General Douglas MacArthur they were eager for action but poorly trained and ill equipped. Yet thanks in large part to strength in numbers and superior aircraft, the US troops quickly pushed the North Koreans north, and over the next two months the war dramatically turned. But on November 26, when a quarter of a million Chinese soldiers joined the fight, the conflict became bloody and the outcome once again grew uncertain.

As it was so different from World War II, the Korean conflict offered challenges unlike any Americans had ever faced in combat. As jets roared overhead, men hid and fought in trenches much as they had in World War I. The armies advanced and retreated on a daily basis. Ground was given up, recaptured, and then given up again. On top of that, the enemy was illusive and hard to spot, and roads were heavily mined. At times, guerrilla fighting meant small forces could hide while inflicting major damage. Then, a few miles down the road things became conventional as waves of motivated attackers charged United Nations' positions. On top of not being able to predict the enemy's moves, radical weather changes made Korea one of the most inhospitable places on the planet. The Allies had to be on watch for every kind of military tactic as they fought in rain, snow, and heat. Because of all of these often-conflicting issues, morale quickly flagged and some questioned the value in waging this action.

As the fighting intensified, World War II veterans pointed out that many of the deaths they witnessed were unnecessary. In the fight against Japan and Germany, scout dogs had saved countless lives simply by alerting units to enemy presence. Now, while fighting on unfamiliar ground, the Americans were at a distinct disadvantage simply because there were no dogs to warn them of possible dangers. Without "dog sense," many suggested, the enemy could sneak up using both surprise attacks as well as well-positioned snipers to pick off men one by one. Thus, vets argued, men were getting needlessly killed on what should have been routine and somewhat safe scouting missions. Sadly, for a while no one listened to this wisdom.

Men dying one at a time rather than in waves had the most devastating effect on morale. When someone was taken down by trip wire, a mine, or a sniper in a tree without a single American shot being fired, it created a sense of helplessness that swept over entire combat units. These deaths also began to cause men to question why they were in Korea. Grumbles of "This isn't our country" and "We weren't attacked" were passed among the soldiers. As the enemy grew more determined and the war stretched out, tired men who had lost many friends were growing more discouraged each day. They felt they were dying and no one was noticing or even cared.

To a certain degree this was true. Back in the United States the news media was not reporting the conflict in Korea as they had with World War II. War stories were not the top headlines. With television in its infancy and newsreel budgets dramatically cut, the general public rarely saw film of battles. And then there was the problem of what could you say about a war where there were no real fronts and no defined objectives. It was all but impossible to describe the kind of action in a way the public could understand. Even as casualties mounted and the price of war personally hit home in more American families, the news coverage did not expand.

As a determined enemy fighting on their own land dug in, the Americans needed a leader who could provide real hope and a battlefield advantage. Many of the top brass kept pointing to new technology as the answer while others suggested it was time to dust off atomic bombs, but a few quiet voices, mainly belonging to boots on the ground, kept pitching a much simpler suggestion that had already been fully tried and tested in combat. In this case the soldiers barked and wagged their tails.

At the end of World War II, the American military had cut back on funding dog-training units. It appeared the armed forces no longer saw canines as valuable partners in combat action. By 1951, only one active duty scout group remained. Those heading the 26th Infantry Scout Dog Platoon, located at Fort Riley, Kansas, were likely not thinking about Korea or combat duty. Essentially they had become an Army public relations unit with a primary mission of conducting dog demonstrations and making television appearances. But with the war stuck in the Korean mud, a call was sent out from Asia begging that dogs be trained for combat duty.

Though the location of the action was far different from Pacific Islands or Europe, the training was similar to what dogs received in World War II. At Fort Riley the four-footed soldiers were taught the skills to recognize anything and everything that might be dangerous. This included hearing weapons being readied for action, the sound of enemy vehicles, and the noise made by artillery shells or aircraft; smelling, hearing, or sighting snipers; and spotting mines.

In these areas a dog's sense of sight, smell, and hearing were far superior to a man's. But while the handlers understood this, many officers couldn't bring themselves to trust the dogs even in training exercises. Thus, the canines were only going to be as useful as those in charge of the military units allowed them to be.

At Fort Riley one dog stood out as possessing skills beyond the rest of his class. York was a solidly built, athletic German shepherd. Tan and black, with a large head and expressive eyes, the canine was one of the few dogs that didn't favor just one of his senses. He seemed to equally rely on his eyes, ears, and nose. Perhaps this was the reason that in every possible combat situation test results proved him to have no weaknesses.

Those at Fort Riley believed that the future of dogs as military partners hinged on how their star pupil York would respond under fire, and the trainers had complete faith in him. Thus, in May, when the 26th Infantry Scout Dog Platoon received orders to embark for Korea with its six dogs determined ready for combat, the canine that was number one in his class was marked for the toughest assignment.

On June 12, the tan-and-black York was assigned to the 2nd Infantry Division of the United States Army. The 2nd made up almost one-third of the American soldiers stationed in Korea. Formed in World War I, the division had been a part of some of the toughest battles in the fight against the Nazis in World War II. Many of those men

were still with the 2nd when the Korean conflict broke out
and were the first to be deployed directly from the United
States to combat. Experiencing the most intense fighting
of the police action, nineteen members of the 2nd would
so distinguish themselves in combat that they would be
awarded the Congressional Medal of Honor. But in spite of
unparalleled valor, the unit's morale was suffering under the
enormous toll suffered in the conflict.

The 2nd had been losing men at an alarming rate
outside normal battle conditions. On seemingly routine
patrols soldiers were dying due to sniper fire, mines, and
surprise attacks by enemies that had managed to steal
behind American lines. Thus, even though many of the
officers were skeptical, York and his handlers were assigned
to lead these patrols. Here is where the validity of military
dogs in modern warfare would either be proved or shown
as an outdated tool to be relegated to history books. Hence,
there was a lot riding on the German shepherd's broad
shoulders.

By going ahead of the forces, York and those with him
were targets. Often working in the open in areas that offered
no cover, York was being asked to sense men who were
completely hidden from view while also noting trip wires
and mines.

Padding along dusty roads and through bombed-out
villages, York's head was up as his gaze constantly shifted
from side to side. As the men around him looked on, the
dog's pricked ears stood high when he noted something

suspicious and his focused eyes directed the soldiers to the problem. Trusting York's senses did not come easily for men who had never worked with a trained dog. When they noted nothing in the direction where York was looking, some grew impatient and moved forward only to have gunfire prompt belly flops onto the hard ground. After only two or three missions, when the dog stopped so did the men.

In his first few months of service, the German shepherd had to deal with the unrelenting heat and by November he was dealing with Arctic cold. He worked in every kind of condition and never once lost his focus. Therefore, York became a thorn in the North Koreans' side. Using his vision, sense of smell, and hearing, he was exposing men that had remained hidden in the past. He was also detecting mines that humans were missing. By Christmas it was estimated the dog had likely prevented hundreds of deaths.

In the rolling terrain, the 2nd was assigned the task of taking hilltops. The job was daunting and the cost in lives was enormous. The North Koreans and Chinese were dug in and well armed in spots that presented panoramic views of the landscape below. While bombing and artillery helped keep the enemy entrenched, it didn't drive them out. The only way to accomplish that was by charging through waves of fire. In those kinds of fights the dog was kept behind the lines. But at night, when the enemy's eyes were impaired, York would quietly lead men up the sides of those hills. Largely using his sense of smell, he would point out enemy positions and allow the unit to engage in unexpected assaults that wiped out entire squads. This made the task of taking the cliffs much easier the following day.

When the sun shown and the Americans advanced, the German shepherd went forward to define probable points where the enemy's position was the weakest as well as nose out other areas that were well fortified. He was also able to help determine supply routes and sense out movements along those lines so the North Korean and Chinese convoys could be taken out before they reached their destinations. This enhanced the American war efforts to delay the enemy resupplying its frontline divisions.

Scouting was also important when injured soldiers were moved to field hospitals for treatment. Having York along meant routes for transporting seriously wounded men were safe and efficient. Using the dog in this way also saved countless lives. Perhaps no dog had ever been worked as hard or as often as York and certainly no dog had ever enjoyed it more. York seemed to live to frustrate the enemy!

By Christmas, York had become more than a tool and emerged as a good-luck charm. When he led the way, no one died. So soldiers began to seek out the German shepherd to have him lick their hand for good luck or petted him hoping that simple action would provide them with a bit of the dog's invincibility. Those fortunate to work close to York also shared their best food with the dog, read him letters from home, took pictures with the canine, and swapped stories with other units of the incredible superdog. The dog became so well known to the friends and family of servicemen that he was placed on church prayer lists and talked about on schoolyards and in sewing circles.

Like a great Major League Baseball pitcher, York actually made his job look far too easy. His gaze was so sharp, his hearing and smell so refined that nothing could surprise him. So when he was casually moving forward, the men could relax. When he slowed or tensed, they were ready for action.

The dog's ability to sense trouble well in advance gave those with him a tremendous advantage. Hence, soldiers asked to be placed with York's unit. In a very real sense they saw the German shepherd as the 2nd's Most Valuable Player. His reputation as a lifesaver grew to the point that by spring every patrol that went out asked for York. While a jolly, outgoing pet during rare down times, when on duty the dog had a singular focus and his concentration was unwavering. Nothing could unnerve him. While worried men always shifted their gaze to the skies at the sound of airplanes, York didn't. He was able to identify the difference in hostile and friendly air traffic by sound. He also knew the sound of enemy tanks from those the Americans were using. Thus, he only reacted if the men needed to seek cover.

Because York had the ability to spot trouble before it happened, he was not fully appreciated until officers began to study statistics. After one year of service in Korea, the Army reviewed the canine corps' impact and made a startling discovery. In units without dogs, more men were dying because of surprise attacks by hidden enemies. In groups with dogs the casualty rate dropped significantly.

And with York leading, no one was dying and few were even being injured. There was no way of measuring how many lives were saved by the dog, but the once-skeptical officers guessed the number to be in the hundreds. Because of this the Army grasped what had always been obvious to those serving with York; he was the canine Babe Ruth.

The American top brass were not the only ones to notice the difference the dogs were making in the war. The enemy was being so hounded and frustrated by the German shepherds that their commanders made the canine soldiers primary targets. Yet the shoot-to-kill orders did no good when it came to York. He constantly sensed their presence before the North Koreans or the Chinese could act. Thus, no one collected the bounty on his head. In fact, because of him hundreds of the enemy died or were captured before they could even act.

In February, the General Orders of the Department of Army, No. 21 was issued. It cited the value of dogs on the battlefield. That order reads as follows:

> The 26th Infantry Scout Dog Platoon is cited for exceptionally meritorious conduct in the performance of outstanding services in direct support of combat operations in Korea during the period 12 June 1951 to 15 January 1953. The 26th Infantry Scout Dog Platoon, during its service in Korea, has participated in hundreds of combat patrol actions by supporting the patrols with the services of an expert scout dog handler and his highly trained scout dog.

The members of the 26th Infantry Scout Dog Platoon while participating in these patrols were invariably located at the most vulnerable points in the patrol formation in order that the special aptitudes of the trained dog could be most advantageously used to give warning of the presence of the enemy. The unbroken record of faithful and gallant performance of these missions by the individual handlers and their dogs in support of patrols has saved countless casualties through giving early warning to the friendly patrol of threats to its security.

The full value of the services rendered by the 26th Infantry Scout Dog Platoon is nowhere better understood and more highly recognized than among the members of the patrols with whom the scout dog handlers and their dogs have operated. When not committed to action, the soldiers of the 26th Infantry Scout Dog Platoon have given unfailing efforts to further developing their personal skills as well as that of their dogs in order to better perform the rigorous duties which are required of them while on patrol. Throughout its long period of difficult and hazardous service, the 26th Infantry Scout Dog Platoon has never failed those with whom it served; has consistently shown out standing devotion to duty in the performance of all of its other duties, and has won on the battlefield a degree of respect and admiration which has established it as a unit of the greatest importance to the Eighth United States Army. The outstanding performance of duty proficiency, and esprit de corps invariably exhibited by the personnel of this platoon reflect the greatest credit on themselves and the military service of the United States.

After two years of constant service, on June 16, 1953, York led the last of his 148 patrols. There were no surprises. Also, as had been the case for twenty-four months, no one died on York's watch. A few weeks later, General Samuel T. Williams, commander of the 25th Infantry Division, presented the German shepherd a Distinguished Service Award. On that day, hundreds from one of the most highly decorated and recognized units in the United States Army saluted York as the member of that group that had likely saved the most lives.

While other combat veterans returned home, York continued to serve in Korea for four more years. Much like he had before the war ended, he led patrols on scouting missions along the DMZ. Thankfully, during this time he was not called upon to save any lives.

In the spring of 1957, the United States Army decided it was time to bring one of the Korean War's greatest heroes home. On the first leg of the flight, York landed in Japan and was greeted by the media, local dignitaries, and civilians. Hundreds waited in line for a chance to meet and pet the dog. His next stop was the Army Dog Training Center at Fort Carson, Colorado, where he was assigned the task of touring the nation to develop interest in the recruitment and procurement of dogs for the military. After being honored in cities across the country, the German shepherd was then transferred to Fort Benning, Georgia, where he served with the 26th Infantry Scout Dog Platoon until his death.

Korea reinforced the value of canines working alongside

men in combat and giving those men an opportunity to not only perform better in war but to have a much greater chance of coming home to their families when the fighting ended. Thanks to York and those that served in Korea, scout dogs would also become key tools during the war in Vietnam. It is likely that thousands more Americans would have died in Southeast Asia if the dogs had not been used as scouts.

As a majority of Americans now only know about the Korean War due to *M*A*S*H*, it seems appropriate that the television series once saluted canine soldiers. In the episode "Mulcahy's War," Sergeant Cupcake, a German shepherd that had been injured in combat, had his life saved by army surgeons. In this episode the scriptwriter fully understood the value of dogs like York and educated the show's viewers on the way those that served with York felt about him as a soldier and a friend. In almost every way Cupcake represented York except that the real soldier dog was never injured. He was simply too smart for those who tried to bring him down!

TEN

HONOR AND COURAGE

You will never do anything in this world without courage. It is the greatest quality of the mind next to honor.

—Aristotle

Today, when most hear the name Nemo, they think of the clownfish in the modern Disney animated classic *Finding Nemo*. Before that, "Nemo" most often conjured up images of the mysterious captain in Jules Verne's *Twenty Thousand Leagues Under the Sea*. But for those who know and honor dog history, Nemo stands out as one of the true heroes of the Vietnam War. Five decades ago, in a time and environment much different from that which we have today, this German shepherd proved his value and grit as a soldier. But Nemo was not born into the military service or seemingly destined for combat. Initially he was an energetic puppy looking for a family to call his own and a fenced backyard to call home. Yet for people and canines, fate has a way of stepping in and changing everything.

Born in October 1962, the black-and-tan German

shepherd pup initially found a home as a rambunctious pet with an Air Force sergeant. When his owner was transferred the dog was not allowed to accompany him to his new assignment, so the sergeant's employer stepped in and drafted the canine. Now a year and a half old, Nemo was shipped to San Antonio and in the heat of the unrelenting South Texas summer he underwent eight weeks of basic training, dog style.

Nemo was evaluated based on instinct, intelligence, focus, athleticism, and temperament and, in spite of being an outgoing, friendly creature, was placed in sentry school. Under the merciless sun, Nemo went through physical training that included scaling fences, dragging wounded soldiers to safety, and identifying the location of men posing as enemies behind buildings, in brush, and hiding in the shadows. He was also taught to understand situations and moods: what kind of behavior represented a threat and what didn't. So while he would always attack on command, he also grew to understand when to plunge forward based upon instinctively recognizing danger. Nemo's uncanny ability to sense a threat pushed him to the top of his class while his large athletic body and lightning-quick reflexes made him as much a weapon as a soldier's rifle. In other words, the draftee showed great potential for combat duty.

Upon graduation from Lackland Air Force Base dog training school, Nemo was sent to a tattoo artist who, as an act to signify his value to the military, inked A534 inside the dog's left ear. He was then dispatched to Washington and assigned to the Strategic Air Command at Fairchild Air Force Base in Spokane, Washington. With Airman Leonard Bryant as his handler, the dog performed routine sentry duties in a relaxed setting in one of the most beautiful areas in the United States. For the moment nothing indicated Nemo would ever face anything more lethal than a lost goat or cow or a mischievous raccoon. Yet not long after experiencing his first white Christmas, the two-year-old dog's job assignment dramatically changed.

By January, action was growing so heated in Vietnam that a call was sent out for additional sentry dogs. As the new year began, Nemo was one of many sent to Southeast Asia. Assigned to the 377th Air Police Squadron at Tan Son Nhut Air Base, Airman Bryant and Nemo were one of several teams designated for guard duty around the strategic facility located in the southeastern section of Vietnam. It was anything but a routine assignment.

The French had originally designed and constructed the airport out of the flat, Asian landscape in 1920. It was used mainly for civilian flights until World War II when the Japanese took over large parts of what was then called Indochina. The Japanese military used Tan Son Nhut as a staging platform for their Southeast Asian operations during the war. In 1945, the facility returned to primarily civilian use. Eight years later, with the surge of communist invasions from the north, the French expanded the facility and used it to launch military strikes. In 1957, American Air Force personnel were sent from Clark Air Force base to Tan Son Nhut to further enlarge the base and then it became the home for the South Vietnamese Air Force. As the war increased in size and scope, the base continued to grow as well.

The area Nemo and his handler were assigned to patrol was flat and open. There were long rows of barracks, a main control tower, hangars for equipment storage and repair, workshops, rows and rows of large fuel tanks, several runways, bunkers, and, as a sign of the brutality of war, a building filled with empty coffins. With its scores of fighter jets, bombers, hundreds of trucks and jeeps, as well as thousands of men, the base was an inviting target. What made the temptation even greater were the hundreds of flights that came and went on a daily basis. By inflicting damage on Tan Son Nhut, the Vietcong would severely damage the Americans' ability to strike.

Because of the liquid nature of the war, sentry dogs were vital in Vietnam. Friends during the day were often the enemies at night. There were no traditional fronts to point to and lock down but rather a never-ending series of guerilla raids that inflicted damage followed by quick retreats. It was a deadly kind of shadow-boxing but in this case the blows landed could be fatal. And because of the advent of television news, the images of the war were being broadcast into American homes each night, and over time those scenes of death and destruction were making a huge impact.

By 1966, the war was causing political chaos at home

and creating great divisions across the country. The antiwar movement was rapidly escalating and protests were popping up on college campuses and in city squares. Through no fault of their own, those seeking to serve their nation were often cloaked in a cloud of suspicion. Hence, morale, which was always hard to maintain in combat situations, was made even more difficult in Vietnam. But when you were drafted, you served. That was true of men and canines.

Sentry dogs were first used in large numbers beginning in World War II. Initially they were employed to protect entry points or patrol around munitions or bases. In times their roles expanded beyond the assigned territory and into the field to seek out the enemy before it could attack. In Vietnam, a war that didn't fit any of the conventional profiles, dogs became indispensable because of their ability to actually sense a silent enemy as it approached.

One of the reasons Nemo had been brought to Vietnam was the tenacity he showed in training. In each of the trials he was both eager and fearless. Dogs that embraced this type of focus and courage were called "guided muzzles." Like a heat-seeking rocket, the dog's nose was always pointing to the spots where the enemy was or had been just a few minutes before. In that way he was warding off trouble even before it happened. Yet as valuable as the sentry dog was, his handler was the key to making a "guided muzzle" work.

Bryant understood Nemo as well as he did any person. He could read what the dog was thinking based on the way the German shepherd moved. A slowing of the pace, a lean into the body, a cocking of the head—all things most would not notice—Bryant picked up on. The chemistry in this pairing was unique and invaluable and Bryant's faith in the dog grew to the point that if Nemo stopped, the man never urged him forward. Even before Nemo pointed to the spot where an enemy was hiding, the trainer would signal to the men that were following that something was just not right. If there was not a team patrolling with Bryant, he would use his walkie-talkie to call Central Security Control (CSC) and let them know Nemo seemed to be picking up on something and to have the men ready for action. Yet, as per rules, no one jumped in to assist the dog and handler until Nemo had actually spotted and exposed the Vietcong. Thus, to keep the pair from becoming easy targets the dog had to be able to pierce the darkness and "see" danger when a human could not.

Much like York, a decorated hero dog that served in Korea, Nemo didn't rely on just one sense. He used sight, smell, and hearing without favoring one over the other as most dogs naturally did. The German shepherd's ability to observe and process was so refined that he fully understood when things were normal and when they were just a degree or two off.

For six months the team spotted potential attackers and stopped a number of assaults before they could begin. Thus, Bryant and Nemo were often cited as being one of the best combinations of dog and man in the Air Force. In July, when Bryant's tour of duty was up and he was transferred back to the United States, a twenty-two-year-old Airman Second Class was assigned to Nemo. For the next couple of months, as they trained and patrolled together, Robert Thorneburg and Nemo would slowly develop the skills needed for each to read the other's thoughts and movement. By autumn the new pairing seemed to have come to the level exhibited by Nemo and Bryant.

As November rolled into December, the bustling base embraced the upcoming holidays. Decorations went up in the mess hall and at local bars. Christmas presents sent from home began to arrive in the mail. Holiday standards were played on the Armed Forces Radio Network and talk turned to memories from the past or the sadness of not being home with family. In a sense it was a bittersweet time when homesickness dug its way into the heart of every man on the base. So there were moments when even hardened soldiers and airmen could lose their focus.

December 3 began as a typical day in Southeast Asia, and nothing about it bore any resemblance to the scenes shown on the greeting cards those stationed at the base were getting from home. For most of the day the war seemed miles away. Planes and helicopters were taking off and landing without incident, wounded from other parts of the country were being brought in for medical attention, but locally there were no bullets flying. At least in one small corner of the world there seemed to be a bit of peace on earth. That was to change just after dark.

With no warning, a large force of Vietcong commandos

made a quick approach through a rarely used area around the outside of the base. The undetected enemy was able to cut fences and make its way through the perimeter without a shot being fired. Their objective was to inflict as much damage as possible at the base and then leave the same way they had entered. The Vietcong were so well prepared and trained that they knew their only hope of completing the mission and escaping was by taking down the base's canine corps. As they moved forward in the shadows they kept their eyes open for the dog teams. As soon as a dog was spotted, they fired. Within minutes they'd put three teams out of commission without an alarm being sounded and by using only minimal gunfire.

In a civilian setting, a few rounds of gunfire would set off alarms, but on this air base, hearing light gunfire was as common as noting the sounds of aircraft. With the dogs silenced and the brief noise of battle mild and distant, it seemed just like another night and for the moment thousands slept with no idea that the enemy was a stone's throw away.

Assignments in hand, the small unit of Vietcong commandos divided into several groups and fanned out across the base. As they quietly moved forward, their confidence grew, but then a lone sentry dog noted movement and began barking. In the night it was difficult for the dog's handler to know if the men in front of him were friendly or an invading force. As he sized up the situation, shots rang out and he had his answer. As the dog and airman dove for cover, a bullet found the handler. With his partner growling, the man reached down to feel warm blood soaking his uniform. If he was going to live he had to find cover. Yet even as he crawled deeper into the shadows, his canine companion picked up on something and demanded the wounded airman look back toward the action. The Vietcong commandos, satisfied they had knocked the airman out of commission, were all going in the same direction. Grabbing his walkie-talkie, the badly wounded airman passed his dog's observations along to CSC. That warning would save millions of dollars in equipment and scores of lives. With the alert sounded, two security policemen, now operating on the information provided by the canine team, charged to a machine-gun nest and waited. When the confident enemy appeared, the Americans went to work. Thirteen attackers died within seconds. As additional security forces massed and spread out across the base, the remaining enemy quickly retreated beyond the perimeter and into the night. With only minimal damage to a few planes, the base remained secure, but the victory had come at a cost: three airmen and three dogs had been killed in the assault.

As the news spread of the attack, a sense of sadness settled over the base. This time those who had died were stationed with them. The trio and their dogs were seen every day, and it was one of those dogs that had kept the base from suffering much more damage and loss of life. Therefore Nemo, who had not been on duty that night, was treated with even more love and respect as many airmen took time out of their day to go visit the kennels. As his head was patted a few even whispered, "We're depending on you boy."

Thorneburg reported for duty three hours before scheduled on December 4. In the glow of the late afternoon sun, he first studied the empty beds of the dogs that had given their lives for the base. He then soberly removed Nemo from the kennel and began a careful inspection. Thorneburg's hands lovingly touched the dog from head to tail, looking for cuts, bruises, or any signs of illness. He also checked the German shepherd's eyes, nose, and ears. Satisfied there was nothing wrong, he then grabbed a brush and spent the next hour grooming Nemo. Finally, when there was nothing more to do, the two sat together and waited for darkness.

As the final ray of the sunlight faded, an apprehension settled over the base. Thorneburg and a now-anxious Nemo silently rose as the truck pulled up to take the dogs and handlers to their duty stations. As the various teams hopped into the back of the truck, there was no banter. The loss each had experienced when three teams had given their lives the night before had stolen the airmen's voices and once more alerted them to the fragility of life. As the truck roared toward the base's perimeter, death seemed closer than it ever had been before.

While the men's hearts ached, Nemo and his four-footed companions were alert but no more apprehensive than usual. As he petted the big dog's broad head Thorneburg reminded

Nemo he was depending on him. On this evening his sincere words were more a prayer than an observation.

As per the assignment sent down by command, the teams would split up and follow the path of retreat the Vietcong had used the night before. The base commanders had to know if the enemy had been driven out or were amassing for another assault.

Jumping from the truck, the teams fanned out and swept the area. In the first sweep, the dogs picked up human scents but found nothing. The second sweep was greeted with enemy fire. With no idea how large a force they were facing, the patrol called for help and dug in. In the short firefight that followed, four Vietcong were killed.

Now fully on guard, the men and dogs moved past the fallen enemy and deeper along the escape route. When a German shepherd pointed his muzzle forward and froze, the airmen knew something was up. After once more calling command, they let the dogs go and followed the animals' lead to a series of small tunnels. They were obviously hand dug, and a quick inspection of the first showed it had been recently used. As the dogs led them to the next one, shots rang out. A short but heated exchange followed. Several hundred rounds later things grew quiet. Moving forward, the Americans shined a light into the tunnel. Four more enemy fighters were dead.

At this point Thorneburg and Nemo were ordered to split from the main group and check an ancient cemetery about a quarter mile beyond one of the runways. The markers were all but hidden by five-foot-tall elephant grass. Alone, under a star-filled sky, with seemingly only the ghosts of those who had died around them, the pair made their way through the tombstones. The area appeared clear, so the trainer stopped for a moment, offering silent words of thankfulness. Thorneburg then looked at Nemo. The dog was as still as a statue, the hair on the back of his neck was raised and his ears pricked. He had picked something up. Was the dog now sensing the enemy had passed through this place the night before or was there someone out there now? Thorneburg couldn't report to CSC until he knew the answer to that question.

Crouching and taking a step forward, his gun ready for action, Thorneburg wanted to push on, but Nemo was anchored in place. The big German shepherd refused to move.

"What is it?"

The dog's quick response was signaled by a couple of short steps to position himself in front of the man before pointing his muzzle forward. Following Nemo's gaze, a tense Thorneburg tried to spot what the dog seemed to know was there. At first he saw nothing, then there was a flash of light and a loud bang. A second later a bullet dug into Thorneburg's shoulder and drove him backward. As the man fell to the ground, the unseen enemy fired a second round. This one hit Nemo in the face. The dog staggered backward, but did not fall.

From out of the darkness four Vietcong guerrillas hurried

to finish the job they had just started. Confident they had the jump on American forces, they had no idea they were about to march to their deaths. Though bleeding profusely from his eye and mouth, Nemo charged the invaders. He knocked the first one to the ground before biting the second in the leg. As the man screamed in pain, the two remaining Vietcong tried to squeeze off shots. But because of the wrestling match between man and dog they couldn't lock onto the target. Releasing his bite, Nemo charged at the remaining two men and took both of them to the ground. As Nemo fought against overwhelming odds, Thorneburg radioed for help. Two minutes later, when American forces arrived, the dog was still releasing his terror on the four commandos.

When the rescue team engaged the enemy, an exhausted Nemo hurried back to Thorneburg. Sensing the man needed cover, the dog laid on top of the injured airman's body and licked his face. Nemo refused to move even after the patrol had taken care of the Vietcong and the shooting had stopped. It took an order from the handler before Nemo stood. The dog slowly wobbled for a few seconds, watching his master being examined, before collapsing.

It was quickly determined that while Thorneburg obviously needed surgery for his wound, the bleeding had subsided and he was not in any immediate danger. Nemo was another story. Using a flashlight, the airman cleaned away enough blood to determine a bullet had entered just below the dog's right eye and exited through his mouth.

With a wound this severe the men were surprised the dog was still alive.

Within fifteen minutes of being hit, Thorneburg and Nemo were loaded into a truck and hurried back to the hospital. As Thorneburg went into surgery, Lt. Raymond Hutson, the base veterinarian, was called. By the time he got to Nemo, the dog was barely breathing. When dealing with injuries this severe and a dog that was having issues breathing, logic and training dictated it would be prudent to put the animal out of its misery. But rather than give up, Hutson went against the book and dug in. Once he had dealt with the massive amount of bleeding, he performed a tracheotomy and stitched up the gaping holes. For the moment this saved Nemo's life, but it hardly dealt with the damage that had been done. The next step was removing the useless eye dangling outside the socket. With that done and the eye socket stitched shut, Hutson was confident the dog would live until morning. Beyond that time frame he had no guess.

Nemo beat the odds. He fought off infection, and when the tracheotomy was reversed, he breathed on his own. For the next few weeks he not only clung to life, he grew stronger. Once the wounds healed well enough for the dog to stand and walk, Hutson realized that unless further work was done Nemo would likely never fully recover. The dog needed skin grafts. If this had been just another dog, it's likely the Air Force would have ordered him euthanized rather than invest in such experimental and expensive surgery. But over the past few weeks, Nemo's story had been picked up by the press. The dog's heroic actions in saving Thorneburg had run in newspapers all over the United States. Nemo was even getting fan letters from little children. In a time when there was very little good publicity coming out of the war, Nemo was a star loved by all and thus worth saving. The surgeries were therefore approved with the Air Force closely following the procedures and issuing reports on the dog's recovery.

By the end of the winter Nemo had healed to the point where he was matched with a new handler and put back on sentry duty. Yet after just a few weeks an infection caused the dog's return to the hospital. For several months he received additional treatment but the infections continued. Essentially Nemo was in another fight for his life against an enemy the dog could not sniff out or see.

In Vietnam, dogs were considered equipment. Once they lost their ability to serve they were euthanized rather than returned home. Nemo would have surely suffered this fate if not for the amount of press and fan mail he had generated. Thus, on June 23, 1967, the Air Force ordered the dog back to Lackland in San Antonio for additional medical treatment and deployed his original trainer to accompany Nemo on his return to American soil. With thousands following his story, the dog and Bryant were welcomed as heroes in Japan, Hawaii, and California. At each stop, a vet was called in to examine the dog and the media was given the opportunity to greet and "interview" the canine hero.

A month after the order was issued to return Nemo home, the dog finally made it to Kelly Air Force Base on a C-124 Globemaster. The head of the dog sentry program at Lackland, Captain Robert M. Sullivan, was there and saluted Nemo as he hopped down onto the tarmac. After more surgeries and the base vet giving Nemo a clean bill of health, Sullivan would take the German shepherd across the United States to share the dog's heroic story and emphasize the need for more military funding to train sentry and patrol dogs. At each stop Nemo was treated like the hero he was. The press coverage was immense, the adoration of fans overwhelming, and the salutes of veterans from several wars stirring. In fact, in a time of great division, the hero dog seemed to be one of the few things that completely united the nation.

When the tours ended, Nemo was retired to Lackland where he was given his own kennel. The Air Force put up a sign outside the dog's home providing the details of his life and the honors that he had been awarded. For the rest of his years airmen training to be dog handlers were ordered to meet and spend time with Nemo. Though not required, he was also formally saluted by most of the war veterans who walked by his kennel.

In December 1972, on the anniversary of the engagement that made him a hero and cost him his eye, Nemo died. For the next few months the Air Force debated how best to honor their heroic canine. Many wanted him mounted and exhibited like a museum piece, but that was deemed unworthy of a hero. Thus, on March 15, 1973, with an honor guard present, his remains were buried at the Department of Defense's Dog Center in San Antonio. Two weeks later, on March 29, the last American troops were withdrawn from Vietnam.

It took more than a generation for the wounds created by Vietnam to heal. Finally veterans who had been ignored or even vilified were honored for their service. Except for Nemo and a very few others, the dogs that served in that war were not brought home. When America pulled its troops out of Southeast Asia the military either euthanized or simply abandoned their canine partners. Thankfully this practice has ended, perhaps in part due to Nemo's story becoming so well known.

Eleven

Friendship

Things are never quite as scary when you've got a best friend.
                                                    —Bill Watterson

It was March 1967 when Colorado native John Burnam, then twenty, stepped off a plane and placed his boots on Vietnamese soil for the second time. In his first tour of duty, one that had seen him badly wounded and evacuated to Japan for surgery and rehabilitation, he had been regular Army. Now he had volunteered to team up with a far different kind of soldier.

On that late winter afternoon, as the strong, dark-haired Burnam walked across the base at Dau Tieng, he fully understood that the odds were stacked against him. He'd seen men shot, he'd been with them when they died, he'd watched their bodies being collected and shipped back home. He had personally felt each of those losses and had therefore come to fully grasp the fragility of life. Thanks to this previous war experience, Burnam was also well aware that the enemy—those whose goal was to push Americans

175

out of Southeast Asia—was not strung along well-defined lines of defense but rather everywhere. The sobering reality was that the Vietcong could attack at any moment and from any angle. So you always had to be on your toes and you also had to have complete trust in those around you.

On this tour the young soldier realized that his job with the 44th Infantry Scout Platoon would make him the first and easiest target in any combat situation. His duty station would be in the open and, when properly used, his canine partner would be the best tool the US forces had in sniffing out the enemy. And because of that simple fact there would always be a price on his and his dog's heads. He was therefore a wanted man, but that was a responsibility he embraced.

Because of the huge weight placed on his shoulders, Burnam needed the best weapon and partner possible—a dog that could sense out everything from enemy positions to trip wires. Therefore the canine had to be smart and alert, observant and composed, energetic but also controlled. If any of these traits was lacking, Burnam and the men who trusted him might die.

The first dog assigned to partner with Burnam was a high-spirited, strong, and vocal German shepherd. The black-and-silver animal was also intelligent and eager to learn. Burnam quickly grew attached to his four-footed friend, and, after extensive training, their first few times out in war zones proved that Timber had the potential to be just the kind of dog in whom a man could place great trust. But Burnam had seen men crack under the pressure of combat, so he knew the dog's real value could only be proved in an intense situation. And on a hot, humid day, Timber was finally placed in that position.

Unlike almost all other military personnel, scout dog teams were constantly shifted from one group to another. So they rarely worked with the same units. Therefore Burnam was endlessly introducing himself and Timber to officers. Sadly, many of those who asked for the scout dog team had no idea how to properly use the man or his canine partner. Those without this experience also had little faith or trust in canine warriors.

With little warning and no time to specifically prepare for the assignment, Burnam and Timber were ordered to jump into an Armored Personnel Carrier (APC)—a noisy, gun-laden, combination tank and truck that rode on tracks rather than wheels—and head out into the Vietnamese jungle. The dog had never seen such a vehicle, much less ridden in one, and Burnam spent most of the trip trying to calm Timber down. Worse yet, when they arrived at their objective, several miles west of Dau Tieng, the handler discovered that the 22nd Mechanized Division had never worked with a dog. They had no idea how to use the scout team. Some in the group even seemed to expect Timber to be able to spot the enemy from the APC. When the four vehicles pulled up to a clearing, the door clanked open, and an unnerved Timber raced out with Burnam holding hard on the harness. As foot patrols formed, the scout team was told to find the enemy that was hiding in the jungle.

Initial reports concerning the Vietcong's location had likely been wrong as the team spotted nothing. A couple of hours later, after a break for water and a meal, Burnam and Timber were on the trail again, this time with men following twenty yards behind. As had been the case since the ride in the APC, Timber was agitated and unable to maintain full focus. Even while knowing there could be snipers in the trees and each step might be his last, Burnam stayed calm as he pushed the dog to work.

In war there are two opposing emotions that fight inside a soldier's head. The first is hoping nothing happens. The second is wishing whatever was going to happen would just happen so that the anxious waiting would stop. The worst moment is when these two emotions collide. On this day it was quiet and a second later the landscape was awash in gunfire. As Burnam hit the ground, pulling Timber with him, the trees were peppered with lead. In response, the APC's machine guns also let loose, their bullets flying just a few feet over Burnam's head.

Grabbing his weapon, Burnam tried to spot the enemy's location but he quickly realized the jungle made that impossible. Meanwhile Timber's barking continued to make them an easy target. Unable to move forward or keep Timber quiet, the man and dog backtracked. Reversing course seemed to be the tonic needed to calm Timber down until the dog stumbled over a dead American soldier. A second later Timber went crazy. To keep his canine partner from running, Burnam grabbed his collar and pinned him down on the ground. A few seconds later there was more gunfire and a still-agitated Timber was hit. A second round clipped Burnam. Now they were both bleeding and had no idea where the Vietcong were hiding.

There are moments in war when desperation gives way to acceptance. While trying to spot a seemingly invisible enemy and protect himself, Burnam was struck by the fact that this could be his last stand. He might die in a jungle halfway around the globe from home with only a German shepherd to note his passing. But the problem with dying was that Timber would have no one to protect him. At this moment the dog needed him, so Burnam had to fight to live not just for himself but for the wounded animal.

Grabbing his weapon, Burnam began to fire. At the same time he held on to a panicked, bleeding dog that seemingly possessed only one goal: to get as far away from this place as possible. As the Americans behind him peppered the jungle with weapon blasts, the deafening noise caused Timber to pull even harder on the leash. It was literally a tug-of-war between man and dog. And then, just as suddenly as it had begun, the noise of war diminished and things were as quiet as a Sunday afternoon on an Iowa farm. Was this a reason to give thanks or a sign that the enemy had knocked out the men and vehicles he'd been leading? If the latter were the case, Charlie, as the Americans called the Vietcong, would soon advance on his position to either kill Burnam or take him prisoner. So the cease-fire brought almost as many concerns as the noise of battle.

Needing to find better cover, Burnam, his hand firmly grasping the dog's harness, crawled toward where he'd left the American unit. As the pair made their slow trek, the handler and Timber came across a wounded GI. Holding the dog firmly, Burnam made his way to the injured man's side. The injured soldier's eyes lit up for an instant, as if thankful to have the company of a friend, but a moment later they only stared blankly. A vibrant life was now just a memory, but Burnam reasoned at least the soldier hadn't died alone.

After retrieving the dead man's dog tags, Burnam, with the nervous and injured Timber at his side, continued to crawl back toward what he hoped was the American position. After what seemed like an eternity, he stumbled into a nest of trees where he spotted reinforcements. Somehow they had beaten the odds and lived, but that hadn't been the case for many of the soldiers they'd been assigned to lead. In a very real sense, the day had been a disaster.

As he was treated for his minor wound, Burnam assessed what had gone wrong on the mission. First the group he had been assigned to guide had no idea how to properly use a dog. Beyond that, training had also not given Timber the needed tools to ride in the APC or be able to cope with the noise of battle. Though it was hardly fair, for all appearances, Timber had failed, and in that way so had Burnam. Yet, at least for the man, a great lesson had been learned. He now realized at times he would have to fully explain to ignorant officers how to use a dog and he would also have to have a dog with much sharper skills. While Timber was a strong, willing animal, based on this episode, his attitude and aptitude seemed unsuited for the role he was being asked to play. With so much on the line, Burnam asked to meet other dogs waiting in the kennels to find one that could offer the handler and the men depending on him a better chance at surviving the war.

When Burnam reviewed the available dogs, he came upon a big, black-and-tan German shepherd sporting huge brown eyes and oversized, erect ears. The eighty pounds of potential fury was initially outgoing and friendly. That was great for a family pet but how would he be in a combat situation? As Burnam put him on a harness and walked him around the base, he observed two things about Clipper. The first was the dog's love and devotion to everyone in an American uniform. The second was Clipper's distrust of locals. He simply had no use for the Vietnamese. If the dog were an ambassador this would have been a huge problem. After all, many Vietnamese were fighting with the Americans. But as Clipper's job would be to sniff out the non-Americans in a combat zone, this trait was one to treasure. The dog's distrust would make him more wary on the battlefield.

As Burnam put the dog through drills, Clipper's athleticism jumped out. The dog could scale fences, race through tunnels, crawl like a lizard under wire, and sprint like an Olympic champion. Tests proved his vision, smell, and hearing were also all remarkable. Also working in his favor was that he seemed tireless. In fact, he would rather drill than eat!

Now being fully aware of the varied demands the dog would face, as a part of training, Burnam and Clipper road on APCs, helicopters, planes, and jeeps. The man exposed Clipper to every loud sound associated with war just to test if the dog could remain focused on his assigned task. Finally, in one of the most intensive elements of training, Burnam worked with Clipper on recognizing trip wires. It was these wires hooked up to explosives that cost countless lives on patrols. If Clipper missed just one then the dog and the handler could be blown to kingdom come.

Beyond training, Burnam spent hours feeding and grooming the German shepherd. He also read Clipper letters from home, shared stories with him, and, whenever he had the chance, took his photo. In a matter of just weeks Clipper became the most important thing in his life and it seemed the dog felt the same way. By the time the canine was ready for duty, Burnam had come to view Clipper as more than a piece of essential war equipment; the dog had grown into being his best friend.

For a scout dog handler, the biggest fear is being picked off while on duty. The second biggest fear is having his dog fail in such a way that it costs men their lives. Hence, the day before going out on patrol there is an added weight placed on all handlers' shoulders. Sleep is often difficult and it's not unusual to see handlers working with their dog hours before departure time.

For the men who pulled duty each day in Vietnam the war was simply unfair. There was really no clear objective. There were also no static rules. Even figuring out who the enemy was could be impossible. After all, many didn't even wear uniforms. And this meant that you didn't know who your friends were. So imagine what was being demanded of the scout dogs. They had to determine if there was someone in the jungle and if that someone posed a risk. On top of that they had to find myriad different devices used for booby traps and smell out hidden caches of weapons. The dogs therefore had to be carefully worked in a job that often took a great deal of time, and this caused many officers to grow impatient and plunge into areas the dogs hadn't cleared. So as handlers were constantly being told to hurry up, the pressure on dog teams was both intense and immense.

Clipper's first days on the job covered almost everything that was required of a scout dog. He made his way to duty stations in helicopters, in trucks, and on foot. He pointed out snipers, hidden weapons, trip wires, and small groups of Vietcong soldiers. Best of all, he did everything that was asked of him perfectly.

In those initial outings Burnam became convinced he'd chosen the right dog. Clipper could focus for hours, he was tireless, he was not rattled by the noise of war or riding in a wide variety of machinery, and he never grew excited in the midst of fire. Yet, except for Burnam, few others realized what an incredible dog they were seeing in action. The reason Clipper remained so unappreciated was that he was never allowed to work with the same group day after day. Thus, the full tally of his large skill set was never really observed by anyone but Burnam.

While the Army might not have been giving Clipper citations, Burnam was. He rewarded the dog with special treats, hugs, kisses, kind words, and lots of love. When dog handlers he knew were either wounded or killed, Burnam also began to realize just what a treasure he had. In a kennel filled with good dogs, Clipper was simply the best.

As the weeks of duty became months, Burnam began to understand there was something instinctive Clipper possessed that few dogs and even most men lacked. The German shepherd seemed to fully recognize that war was a life-or-death game. Therefore, he was completely focused while on duty. He never dropped his guard.

Holidays didn't matter in Vietnam; the war didn't stop for turkey and dressing. And on a hot Thanksgiving Day, Burnam and Clipper drew an assignment as point for a huge mission along the Cambodian border. For an operation requiring this many men there would have normally been several dogs and handlers, but perhaps because of the holiday, this time the entire responsibility of identifying a hidden enemy fell on Clipper's broad shoulders.

As they readied to get on a helicopter and ride to the drop-off point, the soldiers assigned to the patrol gathered in small groups and traded stories about everything from last night's poker games to family back home. These men knew one another well and had grown to become like brothers.

Burnam was an outsider. The men he would be leading that day knew nothing about him and he knew nothing about them. This isolation made the holiday all the more lonely.

Once on the chopper, Burnam took a seat close to the open door. This was not as much by choice as dictated by duty. He and Clipper were required to be among the first to hit the ground, so he needed a key place to launch quickly into action. Meanwhile Clipper felt being by the open door was a gift from heaven. Though he might have been in the army, this German shepherd was all dog when it came to riding in a truck or a helicopter. He always leaned his head out a window, or in this case the open door, and allowed his ears and tongue to flop in the wind. At times he would stretch so far out that Burnam had to maintain a tight grip on the harness just to keep Clipper safely on board. The view from the ground or other helicopters must have been entertaining and likely launched a dozen different conversations about pets back home.

As the long ride continued, Burnam grew tired of having Clipper all but pull his shoulder from its socket and so he allowed some slack on the lead. A split second later the chopper leaned a bit as it turned and the dog's paws starting sliding out the door. It would take Burnam a second to grab the leash and yank Clipper back to safety, and during those moments the animal must have seen his whole life pass in front of him. When his paws were back on the helicopter he looked back at his handler as if to say, "How could you let that happen?" Burnam shrugged and grinned as the shepherd moved safely away from the door. For the rest of their time together the dog no longer showed any interest in a window seat.

Once on the ground, all the men met in a clearing and Burnam was assigned to lead the squad into an area where there had been reports of Vietcong guerrillas. Two bodyguards were directed to cover the dog and handler from about thirty feet to the rear. With his nose to the ground, Clipper went to work trying to sniff out the enemy. For several hours the dog showed Burnam signs of activity, such as recent footprints, but displayed nothing indicating that Charlie was still in the area. Finally, just when it seemed the intelligence had been wrong, Clipper grew still, his eyes fixed on a point where Burnam saw nothing. The handler reported the finding to the platoon leader who sent out a small party to search the area. Thirty minutes later they returned having found no sign of any Vietcong.

While the soldiers were now sure the area was clear, Clipper would not give in. He continued to signal through body language that the enemy was around them. A second search only revealed a lot of footprints along a well-worn trail. Though the dog, through both the look in his eyes and the lean of his body, begged the men to hold their positions, the platoon leader lost his patience with Clipper and ordered the unit forward. Once they were out of the jungle in the open, shots rang out and everyone hit the ground. After five minutes of rapid fire, the area once again grew quiet.

The platoon leader looked back at Burnam and Clipper

as if to acknowledge his error before ordering most of the men back into the cover of the jungle. A scouting party was dispatched to see if any enemy soldiers were still in the area where the initial shots had originated. A few minutes later an officer came back reporting the group had spotted a man-made bunker. It now fell to Clipper to see if there was anyone in the hole. As they were on the way to the spot, Clipper stopped and looked to a tree. Burnam suggested to their guide, a brash young lieutenant, that they needed to bring in someone to examine what his dog had just sensed. The officer ignored the suggestion and continued to move toward the bunker. A second later shots rang out from just a few feet away. The blasts from the dark undergrowth were so powerful the lieutenant was knocked backward into Burnam. As the handler fell to the ground, Clipper leaped forward, knocking off Burnam's helmet while placing his body between the hidden enemy and the handler.

By reflex, Burnam glanced toward the officer. The man must have died before he knew what hit him. Sadly, if the lieutenant had paid attention to the dog, it wouldn't have happened. Yet for the moment there was no time to place blame; Burnam had to find a way back to safety.

There was Vietcong gunfire in front of him and American fire flying over his head. Thousands of rounds were being rattled off with each passing minute. Fifteen feet ahead, he could hear the enemy excitedly screaming directions and behind he heard the more familiar sounds of Americans barking off orders. Meanwhile, Clipper remained quiet and focused, his eyes fixed on where everyone now knew the enemy was. The dog's calm response, which was just the opposite of what Burnam had dealt with when handling Timber, allowed the handler to remain cool as well. As the American forces began to spray suspected enemy positions with artillery fire and as machine guns shredded the leaves off trees, he decided it might be time to retreat.

A minute of crawling found the pair back at the tree where Clipper had all but begged the lieutenant to stop. Glancing up, Burnam noted a dead Vietcong sniper, his body partially hanging off a limb. He must have been spotted and shot after the attack began. Though it hardly mattered now, Clipper had been right; there was danger in the tree.

In time the Americans drove Charlie back and the shooting stopped. From a position by a tree Burnam spotted two men carrying the body of the officer who refused to trust the dog's instincts. Five others died due to the rash young man not acknowledging what Clipper sensed. Initially Burnam was angry, but as they loaded up to return home, dozens of men came back to thank the dog and handler for saving their lives. They now realized that without the dog it would have assuredly been much worse. On the chopper ride home, Burnam stroked Clipper's broad head and whispered again and again how much he loved him.

A few weeks later Burnam and Clipper were out with a smaller group when a local man on a bicycle zipped by. The soldiers simply blew it off, but for some unknown reason Clipper was deeply agitated. Trusting his dog's instincts,

Burnam yelled out demanding the man on the bike to stop. Instead of following orders, the local pedaled harder. There was no way to run him down on foot and there was no reason to shoot the cyclist, so Burnam dropped the dog's lead. Less than thirty seconds later Clipper knocked the man and bike off the trail. When Burnam and the rest of the soldiers arrived they discovered a pouch filled with intelligence materials that included American troop locations. Once again, where men had been wrong, Clipper had been spot on. It was likely scores owed their lives on that day to a dog that stopped events before they happened.

By now Burnam felt he had the smartest partner in the Army. He often referred to his canine companion as radar on four paws. As he neared the end of his tour of duty, now-Sergeant Burnam and Clipper were assigned to work with the 2nd Battalion, 12th Infantry to clear out a section of an old rubber tree plantation and the jungle that ran alongside it. The region had been a Vietcong stronghold and hideout for months.

After flying in helicopters to the area, this time with his dog's head inside the chopper, the group began what was a scheduled three-day mission. As the unit pushed deeply into the thick jungle, the clouding, foreboding skies opened up. Soon everyone, including the dog, was soaked to the bone. Worse yet, the moisture brought out hoards of insects and snakes. That morning Clipper was stung and bitten by everything from ticks to ants to fleas but somehow never lost focus. With the large group of men moving behind them, Burnam and his dog ignored the hostile elements and continued their search. After several hours, Clipper signaled via body language he was picking up on something big. A patrol was organized and sent out. They discovered the dog had sensed a hidden base camp, now deserted but containing a large cache of weapons, mortars, and mines. As they were booby-trapped, the bunkers were blown up. Hence, day one had been a success.

After an uncomfortable night sleeping in the jungle, the patrol once more began their search for Charlie. All went smoothly until Clipper alerted Burnam to something the man could neither see nor hear. A scouting party soon discovered another American unit just a few miles away. After the two groups joined forces, the dog and handler were placed in front and asked to lead the combined units into a small village. Rather than taking a direct route, Clipper zigzagged down the trail. Though likely not understanding why, the men followed carefully in the dog's footsteps.

After securing the town, the Americans moved on in a direction that would take them to a base camp for the night. Clipper once again slowly and carefully made his way through tall grass, along a marked trail, and over jungle paths. Those following him fanned out, each man ready to fall to the ground if shots rang out.

Burnam was observing Clipper change direction when a blast to his right shook the ground. A soldier had roamed too far off the dog's course and tripped a mine. His right leg was all but gone.

As the medics worked on the badly injured man, Burnam and Clipper found cover and rested. The day had been long and hard; Clipper was heavily panting, his paws were sore, and his skin had hundreds of insect bites. Yet, after a chopper arrived and evacuated the wounded soldier, Clipper bounced up, once more ready to do his job.

For the next few hours, Burnam pushed Clipper to guide them back to safety. The dog seemed more than ready to go home, but the path he was choosing seemed completely insane. He would walk a few feet forward, make a quick left turn, walk a few more steps and then make a hard right. Though he saw nothing indicating the reason for Clipper's "little game," Burnam didn't question the dog. Evidently, neither did the scores of men behind the scout team. As the handler glanced back he noted the soldiers were no longer fanned out; they were following Clipper's wild course step for step. When the unit finally arrived at the camp, the weary men in uniform actually cheered. Before they unpacked their gear, many of them rushed over to pet the German shepherd's head. A lieutenant even walked up and saluted Clipper before bending down to shake the shepherd's paw.

"What a dog!" the officer exclaimed.

Burnam nodded, still not grasping what all the fuss was about. As the smiling lieutenant rose, the dog handler was enlightened. "I don't now how he did it, but your dog spotted scores of trip wires. Every time he turned I had my men check the spot Clipper avoided. There were explosives at each location. We marked them so crews could come back to get rid of them. In other words, you and your dog saved my platoon! Who knows how many of us would have died today without that German shepherd. And how many more would have died down the road if those devices had not been spotted."

Burnam glanced around at the soldiers who were safe but wouldn't have been without Clipper. As he studied the smiling faces of men whose names he didn't know, he shook his head. How had his dog smelled the booby traps? Had Clipper heard the singing of the wind on the wires? Had he seen them? The handler would never be sure of the answer, but he was completely convinced the dog had done what no man or machine could.

That night Burnam promised Clipper he would always take care of him. He also assured his partner that he would never forget what the dog had done for him and those who served the United States. Yet on March 14, 1968, that first promise was broken. Burnam's tour of duty was up, and even a soldier who had earned the Purple Heart, Bronze Star, and Legion of Merit medals didn't have the pull to keep the dog that, in the man's mind, had served even more heroically than any soldier in Southeast Asia. Clipper was destined to be given to another handler and another and another and would be worked until he could work no more. Then rather than be retired, Clipper was ticketed to be euthanized. To the US Army the German shepherd was just another piece of equipment.

As the airplane was waiting to take him home, Sergeant

John Burnam tried to find a way to say goodbye to the best friend he'd ever known. With tears filling his eyes and words choking in his throat, he whispered how much he loved Clipper. Then with the dog watching, the soldier hurried away. He would never again see the German shepherd or ever find out what eventually happened to the canine hero.

While Burnam could not keep his promise to always take care of Clipper, he spent decades constructing a plan to fully present to the world the value of the dogs that worked as soldiers in Vietnam. He wrote a book, *Canine Warrior*, telling the often graphic but amazing tales of the dogs of that Southeast Asian war. His book rallied other handlers to step forward and share their stories. Burnam also pushed for legislation to build a monument to the dogs that served in all American wars. On October 28, 2013, The National Monument to US Military Working Dog Teams was dedicated at Lackland Air Force Base in San Antonio, Texas. On that day when Burnam was recognized for all his dedication to this cause, tears filled his eyes, not because the monument he had worked decades to build had become a reality, but because he felt he had finally and properly honored the best friend he had ever known. He wasn't able to fulfill his promise to always take care of Clipper, but he certainly made sure the dog and his service were not forgotten. In that way, Burnam did bring his best friend home from Vietnam.

TWELVE

DUTY

Duty, Honor, Country. Those three hallowed words reverently dictate what you ought to be, what you can be, what you will be.
—Douglas MacArthur

The twenty-first century has seen mind-boggling advances in the technology of warfare. As surveillance tools, drones now have replaced the manned blimps used in World War I and the planes employed in later wars. Drones have also sometimes substituted for soldiers as snipers and planes as bombers. Computers have taken the guesswork out of long-range shelling, and cell phones have superseded walkie-talkies, radio communication, and messenger dogs on the front lines. Yet at a time when mechanical marvels have brought a new age to warfare, canines have actually seen their roles advance rather than diminish. It is the war against terror that has fully shown the real significance and value of military dogs. As their potential has become more fully appreciated, the training of these canine soldiers has also become more intensive, elaborate, and defined. As a part of this new emphasis on military dogs the extraordinary has in many ways become the ordinary and what once required the canine to adapt on the battlefield is now another part of the canine curriculum.

As the roles of dogs have been developed, refined, and even redefined, the number of different breeds used by the military has increased. In that way, the dogs you now see in combat have a great deal more in common with their ancestors who distinguished themselves in World War I than they do with the canines found on the front lines of World War II, Korea, or Vietnam. During those latter wars it was German shepherds and Dobermans that made up the majority of the military canine units. But now, depending upon the nature of the job, there are dogs of all shapes and sizes serving in combat situations. One of the most honored animals of this century is from a line of dogs that few would have even considered worthy of military duties just a generation ago. Buster is therefore an unexpected hero who has made the extraordinary look routine.

Britain's Ministry of Defence Dog Unit has long been renown in its ability to train canines for combat situations. This intensive and evolving school has become even more important in the twenty-first century. As warfare has shifted from nations battling nations along well-defined fronts to small bands of terrorists striking quickly and then disappearing into the smoke, the skills needed by dogs have also expanded. Dogs no longer serve as just trackers or sentries; canine soldiers are now needed for everything from vehicle search to explosive detection. As they have honed their skills, these "sniffer" dogs have likely saved as many lives as any modern military tool. And one of the most famous and successful of all these explosive detective experts is an English springer spaniel trained by the Defence Dog Unit.

As the name would suggest, the English springer spaniel first appeared in the British Isles. Developed as a specialty tool for hunters, the springer was bred to find and flush game birds. Therefore it is hardly surprising the breed exhibits the perfect combination of smell, sight, and hearing needed for that task. Considered an average-sized dog, rarely do members of the breed reach fifty pounds or stand more than a foot and a half at the shoulders. Springers have drooping floppy ears, a medium coat, and long nose, and by nature are excitable, affectionate, outgoing, and highly energetic. It is their boundless energy and ability to scan the landscape that has made them one of England's most famous sporting dogs. Those qualities have also led to the breed being the perfect fit to fight a new kind of war.

Long before most nations were confronted by terrorism, the Irish Republican Army (IRA) was honing this new type of warfare. Planting and using explosives to hit government installations and military bases became the IRA's most effective tool. These acts of terrorism didn't require a lot of men, were incredibly hard to detect, and were almost impossible to prevent. They also filled the English and Irish civilian population with great fear and placed immense pressure on the UK's leadership to give in to the group's demands for complete independence.

As the English military upgraded their equipment and worked on developing new technology to fight terrorism, those at the top also looked beyond the latest weapons to the humble dog. Though a wide variety of breeds were examined, the Defence Dog Unit closely studied and evaluated a dog not normally considered for anything but hunting. As an experiment, several of the English springer spaniels were purchased from breeders and planted into schools alongside German shepherds, Dobermans, and Labrador retrievers. Dog handlers quickly discovered that the English breed's instinctive ability to hunt and spot birds translated well when it came to finding hidden explosives and weapons. After six months of extensive training, where the dogs learned all the various smells associated with bombs, the spaniels went to work in Ireland. Over the next few years the breed's unique ability to identify targets before they inflicted damage and caused loss of life helped to significantly reduce the power of the IRA to terrorize the population.

Not long after Americans were awakened to the power of terrorism with the attack on the World Trade Center and the Pentagon, a one-year-old English springer spaniel was sent for a six-month intensive training in hopes that he would graduate a sniffer dog. Upon completing the course, Buster and his handler, Corporal Nick Lyons, were assigned to duty in Bosnia-Herzegovina. This Eastern European region had been a hotbed for ethnic rivalry since the fall of the USSR. And though the war that had required the United Nations to come in and broker peace was now over, terrorism remained a problem. Buster served the Royal Air Force (RAF) well by detecting explosives hidden in packages, vehicles, and buildings. After two tours of duty Buster and Lyons were honored for achieving a perfect record. Yet, during this stretch of duty the pressures of a war had not really fully tested the intelligent canine. So his ability to perform while under fire was an unknown.

With the war in Afghanistan bogged down and British morale on the front lines and at home sinking lower each day, the Taliban was using terrorism to keep forces from the United Nations off-balance. With suicide bombs, road-implanted explosives, snipers, and quick-hitting attacks, the rogues of the desert were creating problems the likes of which the modern military machine could not fully combat. So the RAF turned to a tactic that helped subdue and neutralize the IRA: canine soldiers. Many of the dogs sent to this rugged desert environment did not perform well in the heat. They tired quickly, and as fatigue set in, they often lost focus. This led to explosives not being detected, loss of life, and falling confidence in working dogs from those who had placed their lives in his or her abilities. Like the words found in a classic hit song, what the British canine units needed most was a hero.

Police Flight Sergeant Will Barrow had been working with dogs since entering the RAF just after graduating from high school. Thus it was hardly surprising that Barrow was notified he would soon be assigned to Afghanistan to help reverse this trend of dogs failing to fully identify the explosives used by the Taliban. Before being shipped to Afghanistan, the RAF assigned Barrow to find a dog that was up to saving lives. As Barrow observed and evaluated recent Dog Defence graduates, he called his good friend Nick Lyons and inquired if the handler knew of any canine possessing the extraordinary skills needed in this new kind of war. The conversation that followed would be the first step in saving more than a thousand lives.

Handlers are very possessive of their dogs. Once they find the right partners, they won't give them up. So Lyons looked upon Buster as more than a piece of military equipment; he saw the springer as a member of the family. Lyons and his "best mate" were then serving on the HMS *Caledonia* and stationed at the naval base at Rosyth, England. It was such routine work that Buster had grown a bit bored. Just like career military men, the dog needed action. Putting his loyalty to country over his personal feelings, Lyons told Barrow about Buster and suggested the sergeant drive to Rosyth to meet the dog. The six-hour trip proved Lyons was a very good judge of dog potential. Barrow immediately discovered that with the work harness on Buster was diligent, devoted, intelligent, and focused. When the harness was removed, the springer was outgoing and playful. In other words, he was more than just a great field dog; he was a true friend.

As Barrow noted the deep bond forged between Lyons and the springer, he felt as if he was watching Fred Astaire and Ginger Rogers dance. They knew each other that well, moved as one, and had complete faith in their combined abilities. So the question became, no matter how good Buster was, did Barrow have the right to break up what seemed like the perfect teaming of dog and handler? And, perhaps even more important, could Barrow forge that same kind of relationship—one that would be essential on the battlefield?

And then there was the breed. In the past Barrow had worked with German shepherds, so adopting the springer as a partner was not as natural as it might have been for other men. Yet as he spent time with Buster, putting the canine through a host of drills and exercises, Barrow came to realize that Lyons's assessment was spot on. This dog was a remarkable soldier and also an animal blessed with great character. If Buster could perform on the hot Afghan sand as well as he did on the cool grass of his native land, many lives would be saved. Yet even as he made the final assessment that Buster might just be the dog the RAF needed, Barrow felt guilty about separating the two friends. Thankfully it was Lyons who insisted that Buster needed the challenge and that the men in combat had a far greater use for the dog than he did.

In order to forge a bond and enlarge Buster's skills, Barrow spent the next several months training the dog to be fully prepared for the dynamic needs of their assignment in Afghanistan. This required the two to be together around the clock. As the weeks passed the man often found himself in awe of Buster's ability to discover weapons hidden in trucks and buildings. More important, the dog also could spot the latest and most dangerous killing machine used by the Taliban: the improvised explosive device.

IEDs were wounding and killing thousands of men in Iraq and Afghanistan. Easy to construct and hide, this new version of the land mine was now the most feared weapon of the war. It blew trucks apart, took tanks out of commission, and, when set off, meant almost sure death for any soldier who accidentally stepped on one. On top of that, IEDs did more than just gum up the war for the military; they were also killing civilians on a daily basis.

In previous wars, metal detectors were the most effective way of locating buried explosives. But the IED often evaded the machine's detection until the soldier manning the unit had literally stepped on the trigger. Therefore the RAF had turned to dogs to search for the deadly explosive devices. The canines proved much more effective than metal detectors but there were so many IEDs buried in war zones that even the trained canines still missed many of them. Thus, dogs often died simply because they stepped on an explosive they didn't identify, and in most cases the handler dearly paid for the sniffer's mistake.

In training, Buster never failed. No matter the type of material used in the IED, he was able to spot the weapon, point to its location, and hold his position until humans verified the existence of the device. Doing this in England was one thing—after all, these IEDs were not going to blow up—but could Buster perform the same job while dodging bullets?

In September 2007, after Barrow was convinced the dog was ready, the team was flown to the warzone. If Buster failed just once it was likely that some of the men around Barrow were going to die. The pressure of knowing this put the weight of the world on the sergeant's shoulders. Yet even in these new and strange surroundings, even with the noise of distant gunfire, the roar of airplanes, and noise of trucks, Buster was calm and relaxed. It was almost as if he didn't have a care in the world.

All combat dogs wear a blanket or vest that identifies their unit. As Buster was led from the truck for his first assignment in the hot Afghan sands, Barrow pulled a vest from his backpack and positioned it on the canine's back. Rather than being a bright shade of red, green, or yellow, Buster's was black. Barrow had been told that killing a good sniffer dog was more important to terrorists than taking down a dozen men. Thus, the sergeant's reasoning in choosing the ominous color was to prevent the springer from being an easy target for snipers.

The first night out, Buster was assigned to study a route often used by Taliban rebels. Because IEDs were so unpredictable and it was so easy to hide them in the sand, even a routine daylight patrol was filled with tension. At night nerves were stretched far tighter, but if Buster felt the tension, he didn't show it. A dozen sets of eyes watched the newest canine jog along the road. Barrow was almost sick with apprehension. This was a far different world than the training field. One wrong step in England meant the dog had failed a test and would not be given a treat. A wrong step here would be fatal.

As the dog padded along on a now-cooling sandy road, he held himself with an almost military bearing. His movement was sharp and crisp, his bobbed tail stood at attention, and his expression relaxed but stern. He was every bit as much a soldier as his human counterparts and at this moment much more exposed. As men huddled in the shadows, a completely focused Buster methodically checked the road. Then, without notice, he stopped and his back legs began to almost dance in place. Barrow fully understood the dog's body language; he'd found an IED. At that moment Buster was called back and the bomb crew went to work. On his first mission the sniffer had uncovered an IED that would have literally blown a truck in half. Amazingly it was so well buried it likely would not have been spotted by most soldiers in daylight, and at night no man would have known of its placement until it was too late. If this was the only explosive Buster ever discovered, he was already an MVP to a half dozen Brits.

Over the course of the next few weeks Buster found scores of IEDs. For a dog trained for this purpose that was not remarkable. After all, several dogs had identified that many during similar periods. What was amazing was the springer had not missed any. No explosive devices had gone undetected on his watch. Yet in the same area, when Buster was not on duty, metal detectors had not detected a number of IEDs and men had paid with their lives.

The Brits and Danes working alongside Barrow and Buster began to see the dog in almost mythical proportions. They quickly gained so much confidence in the springer they reasoned no IED would be left undiscovered along the road with Buster on duty. Therefore there would be no surprises. This allowed the soldiers to focus on all areas of their jobs.

When he was off harness Buster was literally the best friend of every Brit in the region and was showered with treats and hugs. One of the most positive things about life on the front lines in a modern war was that members of the military had much greater access to almost instant communication with family members back home. Via Wi-Fi they could make calls home, have video chats, and share photos on a regular basis. So in the most dangerous regions of Afghanistan, a place where death was always a misstep away, members of the military began to line up in order to have their pictures made with the springer spaniel before racing to call home and share the story of the unit's MVP. For just doing his job, Buster's story was being shared by thousands in the UK.

The fact that the RAF was now much more successful in finding IEDs was not lost on the Taliban. Intelligence reports indicated the rebels had placed a price on Buster's head. With this in mind, Barrow soon became more concerned about the dog being shot than stepping on an explosive. Yet as Buster was so low to the ground and there were so few places for snipers to hide in the open desert, the task of taking him out was all but impossible. The few times the Taliban tried, Buster somehow sensed their presence and alerted the unit. So the springer was not only good at saving the lives of men, he was pretty good at protecting his own skin too.

Beyond finding IEDs, Buster also served as a roadside inspector. The RAF stopped and searched all vehicles they believed might be hiding bombs or weapons. Through visual inspections the soldiers usually found guns, but with Buster in charge the unit found many more. No matter if they were hidden in wheel wells, in the seats, under the chassis, or in fake gas tanks, the springer was able to pinpoint their location. This led to scores of what seemed to be simple herders or local businessmen being outed as members of the deadly Taliban.

Life in the Afghan desert was likely much harder on Buster than on the soldiers no matter how well he served. The environment was scorching, dry, and unpredictable. While the days could be unbearably hot, the nights were often icy cold. Worse yet, a friend you bought goods from one day might be the rebel trying to take you out the next. Working long hours in these conditions was hard on Buster's feet and skin, but unlike so many other dogs that lost focus due to fatigue or pain, the springer's passion for his job never seemed to flag. He was always ready for action and never shrank from duty. He toiled diligently long after men dropped down on a knee to rest.

While in the field, Buster developed a unique way of alerting Barrow of a potential IED. Rather than just hold position and stare at the ground, the dog created a trademark move. Whenever spotting an explosive, he danced. Buster's jig, as it was soon called, became the most welcome sight on the desert landscape. Each dance meant that another life had been saved.

One of the Taliban's strongholds was along the Helmand River. This was poppy country and the opium made from the plant helped finance rebel operations. So it was in this area where Buster was most needed and where his skills proved invaluable. Day after day he located IEDs that were then defused. At checkpoints the dog also caught men transporting hidden weapons purchased through opium sales. As he constantly shifted from one role to the other he never missed a beat or became distracted. Yet there was something more the dog did that made the British soldier's job much easier. Buster was a natural charmer.

When Barrow visited local villages to search for IEDs and hidden weapon caches, the dog's friendly nature made him an amazing and charismatic ambassador. Though the local kids were usually scared of the German shepherds and Labs used by the military, the springer evoked no sense of fear. In fact, kids rushed up to the dog whenever he appeared. During breaks, when Buster was off harness, they even played with him. Thus, the dog became the RAF's most effective public relations tool. Officers encouraged Barrow to allow Buster to work his charms as much as possible. The trainer only drew the line at one thing: treats. As the Taliban had placed a price on the sniffer's head, Buster's food was strictly limited to RAF-issued chow.

From the poppy fields Buster and Barrow were transferred to duty in Kabul. The capital city had become a hotbed for terrorist operations. As the springer was now recognized as the best explosive detector in the RAF, he was assigned to patrol the most dangerous urban areas. There his value was proved once more as he found numerous weapons and hidden bomb-making facilities. During much of the day, when he wasn't sleeping, Buster was cozying up to locals. He was likely the first English springer spaniel ever seen by the citizens of Kabul and for that reason became a rock star. Whenever he walked down the street scores came out to see him. And, as the language didn't matter in this kind of dog-human interaction, Buster began to serve as a translator of goodwill.

While in the city Buster worked with Americans for the first time. Initially the Yanks, as the RAF called them, were skeptical of the dog's ability to sense IEDs and weapons stores. On the first joint patrol, when Buster danced in an area that had already been marked safe, the impatient Americans tried to ignore the dog's warning and march on toward a suspected Taliban location. Barrow insisted they wait until a bomb detection unit arrived. The experts discovered the IED that had been previously missed and

Buster had found what would have likely killed scores. From that point forward the Yanks requested that, whenever it was possible, the British dog accompany them on their patrols.

After hundreds of successful missions, Barrow and Buster were ordered back to England in 2008. After just a short time on friendly soil, the RAF decided the dog was needed back in Afghanistan. So he and Barrow returned to a warzone that was just as filled with danger as it had been a year before. For six months Buster's perfect record was held intact. It was then decided the dog would be shipped to Iraq where IEDs were being used even more effectively than in Afghanistan. As Barrow's time in the military was now up, Buster was assigned to a new handler. The man and dog's final goodbyes brought even hardened soldiers to tears. Yet just as Lyons had once given Buster up, now Barrow displayed his loyalty to country over his bond with the dog.

In 2009, Iraq was likely more dangerous than it had been seven years before. Though hidden among the masses, terrorists were everywhere. Without warning, snipers picked off members of the United Nations coalition. Even more frightening, suicide bombers were able to sneak explosives into highly populated areas by hiding them under clothes. Along with civilians, dogs and handlers had been killed when these bombers were discovered too late. Therefore, Buster was needed to dance his jig before the suicide bombers could reach their destinations. By pointing out human bombers and finding scores of IEDs, Buster's record remained perfect. The dog was seen as so valuable that he would be the final British canine to leave the warzone.

Buster remained with the RAF until 2011. During that time he was awarded the highest honor ever received by a British dog. He was also made the symbol of the RAF Canine Police unit. Upon his discharge Buster was then reunited with Will Barrow. For the final two years of his life Buster would be a family pet.

Unlike most other dogs from previous wars, Buster represented a new type of canine warrior that did his job so well it looked routine. While in the past, dogs had raced through gunfire or jumped on explosives to save their handlers or their units, Buster had saved more soldiers than any other dog in recorded history by simply doing his job better than any of his canine peers. Buster is therefore the model for a new kind of military dog: one that because of intense training can accomplish things even the latest developments in technology cannot equal. And this English springer spaniel did it so easily that it would be only after he finished each of his jobs that soldiers realized they owed their lives to Buster.

Thirteen

Sacrifice

> *Love is sacrifice.*
> —David Oyelowo

Across the globe people know the physical and mental strengths of the German shepherd, but for most the Belgian Malinois does not conjure up a specific image. Slightly smaller than the shepherd, the Malinois is an old breed that has historically been used in herding and guard work on farms. In 2004, a litter of puppies was born in the Netherlands as a result of the breeder intentionally mating a German shepherd with a Belgian Malinois in an attempt to create the perfect canine for military and police use. Because of the Malinois's remarkable vision and loyalty, the breeder sensed that these traits, when combined with the German shepherd's intelligence, strength, and power would produce a superdog. In at least one case it did.

One of those most interested in testing the shepherd-Malinois pups in a working environment was a nation far removed from the Netherlands. The Israel Defense

Force employed dogs for sniffing out bombs, working at checkpoints, and searching for fugitives. The pup they imported to the Middle East from the Netherlands was a female that likely would have been good at any of those things if she had been trained. Yet over the first two years of her life, Lucca was fed and groomed but otherwise forgotten. It would take the vision of a man from a third country to finally realize the breeder had indeed produced the perfect soldier.

Because of the dramatic change in the world climate after the September 11 attack by terrorists on New York and Washington, DC, the United States Marines had beefed up their use of dogs. When the war in Iraq was declared, thousands of canines were purchased and readied for combat missions. This need for military dogs became so great the Marines even contacted breeders across the globe. When it was discovered that the Israel Defense Force had a number of dogs they were not using, the US military sent some of its top trainers to the Middle East to examine the stock. Little did those giving the orders for this mission realize their decision would lead to saving thousands of lives.

On April 23, 2006, US Marine Staff Sergeant Chris Willingham flew into Israel as a part of a dog evaluation team. A good-looking man, with kind eyes, a firm jaw, and a rock-solid body, Willingham went into this assignment with mixed emotions. He had a family back in the States that he missed terribly and the last thing he wanted was to be away from those he dearly loved. Yet, Willingham was also a person committed to duty. He was a career soldier and when his country called, he didn't question the assignment. Thus, though there were other places he would rather have been, the marine was still willing to get to work checking out the potential of this new crop of dogs.

To the trained military handler a dog's value was measured by what the animal could do in battle conditions. Thus, to be a marine, the dog had to possess all the traits the corps demanded of its men. So Willingham had to carefully gauge each dog's temperament, intelligence, instincts, and courage. If he chose the wrong dog, human lives would surely be lost.

As he studied the canines in the Israel Defense Force kennels, Willingham was first impressed with Lucca's appearance. The two-year-old dog might have been a mix between German shepherd and Belgian Malinois, but from her eyes to her ears, she looked like a German shepherd. She also carried herself like Rin Tin Tin or the legendary Strongheart. It was easy to see as she pranced in her pen that Lucca was strong and eager. Her eyes were expressive, and her movement displayed both power and grace. Yet Willingham would soon discover she was also like a rebellious teenager. She fought the leash, refused to respond to even the most basic commands, and was more interested in play than education. When the American asked the men who were in the Israel Defense Force what he needed to do to get their dog to follow directions, they smiled and suggested she might need to be trained.

It seemed that since Lucca's birth she had been all but ignored. She hadn't received even the most basic training. The question became, could Willingham take this ignorant creature, gain her trust, and get her focused enough to learn what was necessary for use by the military? Over the next few weeks, he made it his mission to find out.

There is a time-honored saying, "You can't teach an old dog new tricks," and while this is far from true, it is a fact that devoting a great deal of time to a dog that has not received any training is a risk. So much had been lost in Lucca's first two years that she might now resist the attempts at education, never gain the discipline needed for combat duty, or just quickly lose interest in working. Yet, Willingham saw something in Lucca's dark brown eyes that convinced him the beautiful creature wanted to learn. So he took the chance.

Lucca had likely never before seen a human as anything other than a source of food. She had rarely been played with or shown much attention or love. Thus, when Willingham petted her, she ate it up. When he brushed her, she went crazy. When he hand-fed her, letting her lick his fingers, she all but squealed in delight. Within two weeks their bond was so complete that Lucca was literally the man's shadow.

As a reward for doing basic obedience work, Willingham gave the dog a hard, rubber dog toy called a Kong. Shaped like the Michelin Man, one end made noise and the other end offered a chance for the dog to chew until she got tired. Lucca loved to chase her Kong, fetch it, toss it up in the air, and catch it. She grew so attached to the toy she would quit eating each time Willingham produced it. Thus, the toy became the reward for every new thing Lucca learned. It was the ultimate training tool.

During their time in Israel, Lucca proved herself not just an eager student, but the most intelligent dog the trainer had ever worked with. In spite of being ignored for two years, she also quickly gained the discipline to follow every command on lead and off. A subtle look and she stopped, another and she went forward, a signal or a voice command and she moved left or right. She even learned how to back up. She mastered basic tasks in hours not days and developed a full understanding of complex commands in weeks.

With the basic skills mastered to the point they were now more reactions than following orders, Willingham moved to what was intended as the dog's real job. This would be the training period that decided if Lucca was sharp enough to serve in the Marines or would return to live out her life in an Israeli kennel.

Three years before, Army Private Jeremiah D. Smith became the first American killed when his vehicle hit an IED (improvised explosive device). Smith's death was a sober introduction to a new form of warfare. Since that time, scores of other soldiers had died the same way and thousands more had been disabled for life. After trying human spotters and metal detectors, the Marines discovered that the most effective way of uncovering IEDs was using dogs as sniffers. If Lucca could master this skill she would earn her stripes.

Knowing the price American military men and women were paying in Iraq, Willingham pushed Lucca far beyond normal military dog training. He had to. IEDs were growing more sophisticated with each passing month, so soldiers' lives depended on the canines finding these hidden bombs before a soldier stepped on one.

From that point forward, Lucca had to be completely focused on her job. When working she couldn't relax for even an instant. Lucca was worked day and night as she learned the smells associated with bombs and weapons she had to identify and uncover. If she missed even one of the places Willingham had placed the scents, if she failed to find a gun or a weapon on a truck or hidden in a structure, she had to repeat the task again and again. She would not get to play with her Kong until she had mastered each new exercise. After a couple of months of intense work, and Lucca passing test after test, Willingham had complete trust in the dog and her abilities. With one phase of training completed, he snapped on Lucca's lead and boarded a plane to the United States.

At Lackland Air Force Base in San Antonio, Texas, Lucca was officially inducted into the United States Marine Corps. She was then given her dog ID, K458, which was tattooed into her ear. After going through a battery of health tests and being spayed, she and her trainer hopped onto another airplane to the Yuma Proving Grounds. In this hot American desert, the dog would be exposed to conditions much like she would find in Iraq. How she performed here would determine her next assignment.

Rudd Weatherwax, the famous Hollywood dog trainer who gave the world Lassie, once noted that the dogs he used in movies had to have a lot more education than a pet. His dogs thus went through the canine equivalent of grade school, junior high, high school, and college before being placed on a TV or movie set. Though different skills are taught, most military dogs received about the same amount of training as Weatherwax gave his canine actors. Yet because so many lives depended on how Lucca worked in combat situations, Willingham took his dog partner much further. By the time he was finished, the Netherlands-born canine had earned not just her stripes but the equivalent of a PhD. She was literally the top dog in her class.

In 2007, Lucca returned to the Middle East as a much different animal than when she'd lived in Israel. As a marine she was now an instrument of war. Her task would be to sniff out enemy weapons, and Willingham was almost sure she was ready to fulfill that task. Yet he couldn't have complete faith in his dog until she was placed into real action. Missing a smell in training meant she wouldn't get to play with her favorite toy. Missing an IED in Iraq meant that she and those around her would likely die. So a lot was riding on this man's ability to train his dog.

Though they had dealt with hot days in Arizona, the heat in Baghdad was like nothing the dog or man had ever experienced. Stationed at Camp Slayer, the dog team faced days when it felt like 140 degrees. On top of that, the terrain was bleak and the mission convoluted. This was now a war with no rules or uniforms. The enemy was made up of hidden bands of terrorists who looked no different from the people who shopped in markets, ate in local cafés, or delivered goods to the camp. You simply couldn't tell friend from foe.

Iraq was also strained by ancient tribal rivalries. These groups had been somewhat united and restrained under the past leadership but were now fighting for spots in the new government, military, and society. The landscape changed on a daily basis as to who had the advantage in each of these areas. The only sure thing was that Iraq was not a safe place for Americans.

Willingham and Lucca's main focus would be finding IEDs. These modern mines were killing machines and unlike in direct combat—where they would be facing American fire—the terrorists could manufacture and distribute these bombs without having to put their own lives on the line. And when someone drove over or stepped on one, the results were horrifying.

Iraq was also a struggling nation awash in weapons. Thus, simply by using caches of what were once Iraqi military supplies, the terrorists could create and distribute thousands of the IEDs. Though the media largely focused their stories on what these hidden weapons were doing to the American military, those walking along streets, visiting hospitals, and looking through cemeteries could also understand the toll this new generation of land mines was having on the civilian population. Those who distributed the IEDs saw this collateral damage as working to their advantage since the local population knew the weapons were there because Americans were patrolling Iraq. Thus, even though the United States was attempting to help Iraq gain security and freedom, to many citizens the liberators were also the problem. If the Americans left it seemed likely the IEDs would no longer be made and buried.

In a very real way Lucca was there to save all lives— not just those from the American military. She identified explosives that killed with no regard to sex, age, or citizenship. Hence, civilians as well as those in the American military saw her with kind eyes. So Lucca quickly became more than a marine, she was also an ambassador. More important, within weeks of arriving in Iraq she was seen as an instrument of hope.

In the past, handlers had worn different uniforms and colors in order to stand out from the other members of their units. But as Lucca and other sniffer dogs began to find more and more IEDs, terrorists put bounties on their heads. With that in mind, Willingham and other canine handlers lobbied to end the practice of wearing unusual garb and to instead, for their safety and that of their dogs, dress like normal marines. As the canine corps became more and more valuable, and as snipers began to take aim at both the dogs and those handling them, the military changed the policy that made them easy targets.

The fact that Willingham was now dressed just like everyone else and Lucca worked off lead gave snipers fits. With her tan coat, the dog easily blended into the environment and the fact she wasn't on a harness or directly beside her handler meant she was all but impossible to spot. So unless they noted Willingham calling out an order or signaling to Lucca, the snipers couldn't find the handler and follow him to the canine. It was a winning combination that, based on logic, likely should have been a part of military routine well before Iraq.

Lucca's ability to work off lead led Willingham to try something new. He affixed a receiver/speaker to the dog's collar and used a microphone to softly give her orders on which way to turn, when to stay, and when to move forward. Amazingly she worked perfectly using the technology and thus greatly enlarged the area the team could cover.

With her nose down, body relaxed but on the move, tirelessly searching, following each command, Lucca was a machine, but she was also much more. Not only did she save lives, she also brought joy. Back at the base the marines who depended on her while on duty hugged her like she was their child. She was given presents and treats and asked to pose for pictures that were quickly emailed back home. If all the attention received turned her head, it didn't show. The next time she was called for duty she was immediately back in top form finding IEDs as well as weapons and explosives in vehicles and buildings. Only when Lucca declared an area free from danger did the marines fully relax.

Lucca did her job so well and made it look so easy that some locals reasoned she had powers and abilities far beyond any dog in Iraq. As the marines in various units began to total up how many lives her "sniffing" had saved, she was treated like royalty. While she was remarkable, essentially she could find IEDs and nose out everything from weapon caches to suicide bombers because Willingham's training had been that good. Without the man's vision, she would likely still be in a kennel in Israel.

For five years and two tours of duty in Iraq, as well as time spent on base in the United States, Lucca's only handler was Willingham. But when the sergeant received the opportunity to be transferred to Finland and have his wife and two children join him on the assignment, it came time for the Marine Corps's top dog team to be broken up. Through the four hundred missions the two had worked, no one had ever been injured by an IED. It was a record that no other American dog team in this war could come close to claiming.

With deep regret Willingham handed Lucca off to Corporal Juan Rodriguez and watched as the two departed for a tour of duty in dangerous Afghanistan. With her new handler by her side, Lucca found herself teaming with the famed Green Berets. As had been the case in Iraq with Willingham, Lucca's work with Rodriguez was so remarkable and her ability at finding weapons and IEDs so amazing that she quickly emerged as both savior and mascot. Her legend grew to the point that if you were with Lucca you were completely secure no matter where you were. With her nose to the ground and her eyes forward, everyone was sure she would spot any and every danger and uncover weapons that even highly trained men and women missed. If perfection had a name it was Lucca. She had your front, back, and sides.

On March 23, 2013, while out on patrol with Rodriguez and several other marines, Lucca did once more what many had now come to take for granted. While walking well ahead of the unit, her nose to the ground, she cautiously approached a spot along the road, stopped, and with her body language indicated the presence of an IED. After being called back to Rodriguez's side, the explosive team went into the area and set to work. It was determined the best way to handle this IED was to detonate it. The explosion rocked the area, shaking buildings and stirring up a massive cloud of dust, as well as causing battle-experienced men to wince and be left temporarily deaf.

As the dust began to clear, Lucca went back to work. Perhaps the massive detonation had dulled her hearing and sense of smell or maybe after years of difficult work, her abilities were beginning to slip, but no matter the reason, for the first time in her life she made a mistake.

While patrolling many yards in front of the unit, with Rodriguez carefully monitoring her every step, Lucca confidently moved forward, showing no signs of spotting any other IEDs. As the marines began to relax, the dog took a step and a split-second later a rumble gave way to an eardrum-splitting explosion. In horror, the handler and those around him watched Lucca ejected into the air by a blast that would have likely destroyed a truck. For a moment it seemed like she hovered and then she disappeared into a cloud of dust.

Those who witnessed the blast knew they should hold their positions. Snipers might have been waiting for the explosion to lure the Americans out into the open. On top of that, where there were two huge IEDs, there were likely others. And now with their best detector down, the marines had no idea where those charges were hidden. Yet Rodriguez and his comrades didn't even wait for the dust to clear. Many of these men owed their lives to this dog; now they had to see if they could save hers. With no regard for personal safety they began to move toward the fallen soldier.

Lucca was first and foremost a marine. Willingham had noted her determination and grit in the first days he'd worked with her. As long as she had breath in her lungs, she would not stop. So even before the men reached her, the dog emerged from the dust and limped back toward Rodriguez. Her first act was to position herself between the IED and the handler. As the amazed marines looked on, the badly injured Lucca continued to try to be of service to them.

A medic got to the dog at the same time that Rodriguez wrapped his arms around her. Lucca smelled of burned flesh and was covered in blood. She had deep wounds on her chest and was missing the paw on her front left leg. A tourniquet was applied to ease the bleeding and at the same time the unit's commander called for a helicopter. The pain she had to be experiencing should have rendered her unconscious, yet her eyes looked toward her handler as if to say, "I'm sorry I screwed up."

As he waited for his dog to be airlifted to a medical center, Rodriguez was awash in guilt. He genuinely felt he had let both Lucca and Willingham down. A man who loved Lucca as if she was one of his children had given her to him for safekeeping and he had failed. How could Rodriguez face Willingham with Lucca's blood on his hands?

With her head in her handler's lap, the chopper rushed Lucca back to the base hospital. After a thorough exam Rodriguez was given the word that baring some unforeseen complications the dog would live. They would allow her to rest overnight and then move her to a human hospital in the morning where she would undergo an operation to determine just how much of her leg could be saved. The vet then suggested Rodriguez get some sleep. While the marine would follow that order, it would be in a manner that was completely unexpected.

Now under heavy sedation, Lucca was placed in a kennel cage at the animal care center. After cleaning up and making a phone call, Rodriguez joined the dog. Taking a Magic Marker he wrote "Semper Fidelis" on Lucca's collar, and with tears filling his eyes he saluted the animal. He then climbed into the kennel cage to spend the night beside her. Later a visitor to the kennel observed Rodriguez and inquired about the reason for the man's deep devotion to the animal. When he was told Lucca's story he remarked, "Sometimes it takes a dog to remind us of our humanity."

The next day, just before the surgery, Rodriguez tracked down Willingham in Finland. The first thing he did was to apologize for letting Lucca's first trainer down. Willingham would have none of it. While deeply pained that his former dog had been so badly injured, he assured Rodriguez what happened was hardly his fault. Together the men prayed that somehow Lucca would survive.

In the operating room, Lucca was treated with the same degree of respect and care as any wounded marine. Her wounds were judiciously evaluated and various possible outcomes and techniques were discussed. The surgeons even consulted with experts in the quickly evolving area of animal prosthetics and only then was Rodriguez called in and presented with the very limited options. Lucca's leg would have to be amputated in such a way that the entire shoulder would be removed. Thus the dog would have to learn to walk on three legs. The only other option would be to put Lucca down. Rodriguez naturally chose the former. In combat the trainer had watched her constantly adjust to different situations. He was sure, even though it might take some time for her to bounce back, that she could and would handle this challenge just as well.

After successful surgery and some time in the ICU, a flight to Germany gave more experienced veterinarians a chance to study the dog and do additional treatment. As the drugs wore off, a seemingly unfazed Lucca stood. As Rodriguez steadied her, the dog took a step forward. Within an hour she was balancing and walking without aid. She was also grinning as if to say, "No problem!"

From Germany Lucca and Rodriguez flew back to

California and Camp Pendleton. As she arrived at the Marine installation she was greeted as a hero. It was determined that a combat veteran of her status should be allowed to stay on the main base rather than be housed in the kennel area. Over the next few weeks, as her wounds completely healed, she was treated with the respect usually shown only to officers. Nothing was deemed off-limits. She had the run of the base.

When given her discharge papers, Lucca was handed back to her original handler, Chris Willingham. The marine, along with his wife and two children, adopted the military veteran as their pet. Yet, due to Lucca's hero status, she didn't get to settle down for very long. Seizing upon her fame, the Marine Corps dispatched Lucca and Willingham on recruiting tours. During these cross-country treks she traveled first class on airplanes and stayed in the best hotels. She was saluted, offered the finest dining, and honored everywhere she stopped. Though Lucca was not a purebred canine and thus had no papers, she was still honored by the American Kennel Club. And even though she was not English, she was also awarded the Dickin Medal, Britain's highest citation for valor by a military animal. Several marines even presented the dog an unofficial Purple Heart as a way of recognizing her sacrifice in combat. Yet perhaps her best work involved her visits to military hospitals to meet men and women who had lost limbs in battle. Thus, while once she was saving lives in combat, she now was providing hope and inspiration to go on with life.

An English newspaper wrote, "Lucca has become a symbol of hope and inspiration to many as she attends military outreach functions, wounded warrior hospital visits and parades championing the dedication and efforts of all service animals....Everyone has embraced Lucca. They mob her on the streets and hug her and take photos with her. She has even had paparazzi following her around London."

Lucca's path to heroism could not have been predicted. Without the perceptive vision of Chris Willingham, the dog would likely have spent her life in a kennel in Israel. If that had been the case she would have never been given even the most basic training. She also would have never felt the devotion or love of a human being. She would have lived and someday died without ever serving a real purpose. Yet, thanks to Willingham's insight and remarkable training, through more than four hundred missions not a single marine was injured when this dog was on duty. And today, countless men and women are alive thanks to a dog that was almost overlooked.

Best-selling author Maria Goodavage has penned Lucca's complete story in a wonderful book called *Top Dog*. To fully appreciate this canine hero's life as well as the potential of all dogs, Goodavage's book is a must-read.